The Gift of Ethics

D1417202

The Gift of Ethics

A Story for Discovering Lasting Significance
in Your Daily Work

TREVOR GEORGE
HUNSBERGER BECHTEL

CASCADE *Books* • Eugene, Oregon

THE GIFT OF ETHICS
A Story for Discovering Lasting Significance in Your Daily Work

Copyright © 2014 Trevor George Hunsberger Bechtel. All rights reserved.
Except for brief quotations in critical publications or reviews, no part of
this book may be reproduced in any manner without prior written permis-
sion from the publisher. Write: Permissions, Wipf and Stock Publishers,
199 W. 8th Ave., Suite 3, Eugene, OR 97401.

Cascade Books
An Imprint of Wipf and Stock Publishers
199 W. 8th Ave., Suite 3
Eugene, OR 97401

www.wipfandstock.com

ISBN 13: 978-1-62564-425-1

Cataloguing-in-Publication data:

Bechtel, Trevor George Hunsberger.

   The gift of ethics : a story for discovering lasting significance in your
daily work / Trevor George Hunsberger Bechtel.

   viii + 96 pp. ; 23 cm. Includes bibliographical references.

   ISBN 13: 978-1-62564-425-1

   1. Christian ethics. 2. Happiness. I. Title.

BJ1251 B375 2014

Manufactured in the U.S.A.

Contents

Preface   *vii*

ONE

Happiness   1
An Introduction to the Good Life

TWO

Decisions   13
Giving Our Life to the Glory of God

THREE

Gifts   25
Ethics in an Ancient Hebrew Worldview

FOUR

Paradigms   41
Learning How to Be Good

FIVE

Practices   59
Working Towards a Goal

SIX

Imagination   71
Living into the New Possibility with Christ

SEVEN

Rules   79

Contents

Formal Ethics in Christianity

EIGHT
Righteousness   89
Filling Our Hunger

Bibliography   95

Preface

These materials were originally prepared for a new course at Bluffton University called Introduction to Biblical Worldview. The course targets all new Bluffton students and attempts to introduce them to the study of Christianity through attention to the ways that Christians practice their belief through studying the Bible, theology, ethics, and ministry. The course has been team taught for seven years by all of the members of Bluffton's religion department. I'd like to thank these people for their excellent work on this course over the years: Jackie Wyse-Rhodes, Randy Keeler, and Laura Brenneman. I'd especially like to thank Alex Sider who came to Bluffton ready to teach the theology portion of the course by meditating on the Lord's Prayer in the Sermon on the Mount. While Laura and I had the idea to focus the course as a whole on the Sermon on the Mount, that these reflections on ethics are focused on the Beatitudes is due to Alex's attention. I'd also like to thank the many students who have read these chapters in draft form, written essays on them, and reacted to them in class discussions. Sam Wildow, Sam Griffith, and Mary Schrag deserve special mention for helping in the editing process. The writing of this book was partially underwritten by a grant funded by the Lilly Endowment through Bluffton's Pathways program. I am grateful to Sally Weaver Sommer and Rory Stauber for facilitating this support. Rodney Clapp and everyone at Wipf and Stock have long been more supportive of my work than they have any reason, Christian or otherwise, to be. I am deeply grateful for the honor of working with them.

Although they do not play a large role in the text, my family looms large behind many of these stories. My parents, Grace and

Preface

George Bechtel, and my sister, Gini, have in many ways made this book possible, and my deepest gratitude is to them. Susan Hunsberger plays a larger role in the text as I have shared my life with her for twenty years now. She is incredible and I owe her so much that I can't begin to relate it.

My teachers at Loyola, Canadian Mennonite Bible College, and Grebel and my colleagues at Seabury and Bluffton, my fellow congregants at Wanner, Charleswood, Chicago Community Mennonite Church, and Shalom—the communities of my own learning—have almost always given me schools of love in which to practice my art, mentoring me into a better version of myself.

I dedicate this book to one of these mentors, Mike, whose story is told here, at least in part.

ONE

Happiness

An Introduction to the Good Life

"Happy are those who mourn,
for they will be comforted."

MATTHEW 5:4

The Beatitudes, a set of short statements that Matthew reports Jesus as saying at the very beginning of the Sermon on the Mount, will form the backbone of this section on ethics in a biblical worldview. Each one of these statements is about a person or group of people who are surprisingly happy, as in the Beatitude which opens this chapter. At least as far back as the Greek philosopher Socrates, happiness has been at the heart of how wise people have understood ethics.

My favorite story about happiness is told in the film *Life Is Beautiful*. It is a story about an Italian Jewish family in the Second World War. In *Life Is Beautiful* the family has much to mourn, but through the father's persistent happiness his son is able to find comfort. I believe that stories are the most useful way for us to begin to learn about ethics in a biblical worldview. I believe this because I believe that the Bible is itself first and foremost a story, and if we want to think about the Bible, we need to learn to think in stories.

In the rest of this chapter I want to tell this story and connect it to Jesus' Beatitude about mourning and comfort. I also want to introduce the rest of this section of the book. First, let me say a bit more about the thesis of this chapter, which I'll restate here: *I believe that stories are the most useful way for us to begin to learn about ethics in a biblical worldview.* In order to demonstrate this thesis, I need to show you why I believe stories are important. This is a question of the authority of stories. I should also be able to show you that stories do help us learn by example. I should be able to tell you a good story and show how it connects to ethics. I follow Socrates in believing that happiness is the heart of ethics. *Life Is Beautiful* is a good story for the purposes of my thesis, because it is a story about happiness and also a story with more than one worldview. In this way it serves as a good metaphor for a biblical worldview.

Introduction: Believing with/in Authority

Stories other than *Life Is Beautiful* might be useful too, but I believe that we need to think in terms of a story when we are learning about a worldview. Worldviews are stories that we tell ourselves about our world. I also believe that as often as we can, we need to let ourselves be guided by stories when we are trying to be ethical. In particular I believe that stories are more useful than goals or rules for the person or community who is trying to be ethical. I believe this because I believe that only stories have the richness to help us think about the complexities in our lives. Stories have the strength to sweep us up in their narrative or flow of events so that we can imagine ourselves actually living in the story. In addition to being strong in this way, stories are also noncoercive. That is to say that a story very rarely forces us to think or believe or do anything. Stories are so useful for people who want to think about ethics, because they are strong (complex) and voluntary (noncoercive).

Not everyone believes that stories are so useful for ethics. As I hint above, there are at least two other ways (goals and rules) of thinking about ethics in reference to the Christian religion. We'll explore these in more detail later. For now I simply want to note that while I am stating what I believe to be true, other reasonable people disagree; furthermore, I cannot prove (in what we might call a mathematical or scientific sense) that stories are at the center of ethics. The world of ethics is not black and white. Does this mean that there is then no truth or that truth is merely a private matter so that what I believe is true for me but cannot be made to impinge on other people's lives? This is an important question, and we will take it up again and again in different ways in the chapters that follow in this section. For now let me state simply that you, the reader, and I, the author, work together as a community of sorts to create truth. We are responsible to each other. Of course, this extends far beyond you and me. At the limit everyone who learns about or attempts to inhabit a common worldview has a responsibility to each other to consider the truth he and she share.

Therefore, the claim that stories are the most useful way for us to think about ethics is a claim that I am making and you are reading, and it is an important claim which attempts to ground our reality. The way that the Gospel writer Matthew begins and ends the Sermon on the Mount is a good example of the strength and voluntary nature of stories:

> Now when Jesus had finished saying these things, the crowds were astounded at his teaching, for he taught them as one having authority, and not as their scribes (Matt 7:28–29).

It is interesting to note that nowhere in the Sermon on the Mount does Jesus claim authority for himself. He simply speaks as if he has authority. It is not Jesus who claims authority, or the disciples who claim authority on Jesus' behalf; however, Jesus does have authority at the end of the Sermon on the Mount, for the crowds give it to him in their astonishment. Jesus works together with his audience to establish his claims.

Of course, Christians do not simply believe that Jesus was a good teacher. Christians believe that Jesus is the Son of God. Interestingly, Jesus himself, at this point in the story, is not particularly interested in having the good news that he is the Son of God spread about. Matthew reports:

> When Jesus had come down from the mountain, great crowds followed him; and there was a leper who came to him and knelt before him, saying, "Lord, if you choose, you can make me clean." He stretched out his hand and touched him, saying, "I do choose. Be made clean!" Immediately his leprosy was cleansed. Then Jesus said to him, "See that you say nothing to anyone; but go, show yourself to the priest, and offer the gift that Moses commanded, as a testimony to them." (Matthew 8:1–4)

Teaching is something that anyone can do. Jesus teaches with authority and lets the crowd, with their own reaction, give credibility to his teaching. Healing is something that only God can do. It might be the proof that Jesus' teaching is God's teaching. I have spent so much ink on belief and authority at the very beginning of this section because I believe that it is very important to recognize that Jesus is more interested to have the crowd validate his teaching than to validate it himself, even though he could have! Jesus, even when he acts with authority at this point in the story, is not interested in having people blab about it. I believe that Jesus is also interested in working with his audience to create truth.

In fact, we get another clue to this at the very beginning of the Sermon on the Mount:

> When Jesus saw the crowds, he went up the mountain; and after he sat down, his disciples came to him. Then he began to speak, and taught them, saying . . . (Matthew 5:1–2).

Note that it is not at all clear to whom Jesus is about to preach. There are crowds, and Jesus goes up a mountain (so that they can hear him? or at least see him?). There are also the disciples who come to Jesus. Jesus could be teaching the crowds, but why then does Matthew report that the disciples come to Jesus? Jesus' teaching could be just for the disciples, but then why does he teach when there are so many people around? It is likely that Jesus aimed his teaching at the disciples but was happy for any in the crowd who wanted to listen to hear for themselves. In some ways Jesus has a double audience. He is a bit like a tour guide in a museum who does not mind attracting a crowd of nonpaying guests who voluntarily want to learn.

In this way, when I state that stories rather than rules or goals are where we should look to for authority, I recognize that I must convince you of my thesis. You may be convinced or you may not be convinced. In a very real way we are looking at the question of ethics in a biblical worldview together and are responsible to each other in this process. The material in these chapters is my best attempt to truthfully convince you about what I believe the best way to live a human life is, the best way to be happy. I hope that in your reading you will hold me accountable to that high goal. With this introduction in hand, let us move together to my favorite story about happiness.

Happiness in a Concentration Camp

We return to *Life Is Beautiful*. As Jews trapped in the holocaust, Guido and his son Joshua find themselves on a train from Italy to Germany, facing likely extermination in a concentration camp. Their uncle Eliseo is immediately gassed upon arrival. Guido hides Joshua from the Nazi guards and then works to convince Joshua that life in the camp is really just a game. The rules for game are these: if Joshua cries, complains that he wants his mother, or complains that he is hungry, he will lose points. Quiet boys who hide from the guards earn points. The person who wins the game will win a tank.

The stage is set; Guido and Joshua are in what is surely one of the saddest places our world has ever seen, but Joshua is primed to think that this is a game. Even though they are surrounded by sickness, misery, and death, Guido gives such a good performance that Joshua experiences the camp as one of the most fun experiences of his young life. When the guards yell at the prisoners, Guido "translates" their commands into instructions in the game. When Joshua despairs at his situation and asks to quit the game and go home,

Guido lifts his spirt by telling him he is in the lead. At the end of the movie, Guido is led by the German prison guards to his execution. With Joshua watching Guido comically mimics the actions of the guards, much to Joshua's amusement. American tanks roll into the camp soon thereafter, and Joshua wins this game.

Happiness can mean many things to many people. It can be a state of contentment, humor, or amusement. In this story it is also an activity. Guido works very hard at happiness, perhaps for himself, but surely for Joshua. Everything he does has the goal of creating, maintaining, and sustaining Joshua's happiness. Joshua is willing to trust his father's explanation that this concentration camp is, in fact, a happy place or, at the very least, a place where a fun, if very weird, game can be played. Joshua's trust that his father understands what can count as happiness is what I think makes *Life Is Beautiful* so beautiful. That trust animates the world that his father is creating for him. The world that Guido creates is on one level deceitful—concentration camps are not happy places—but on other levels it is more truthful than the concentration camp itself. That is, and this is I think the important lesson that we can learn from *Life Is Beautiful*, happiness is not so much dependent on the harsh realities of our situation, nor is it a simple emotional state that we simply will (as if we can decide whether to be happy or not); instead, our happiness is connected both to our actions and to the actions of those around us. For Joshua happiness is the activity of trust.

What is happiness then for Guido? Guido must also experience many other feelings (despair, anger, mourning), but he rigorously maintains an amused attitude. This is certainly partly because it is necessary in order to build the fiction of the game up around Joshua, but it also seems that Guido is authentically and constitutionally a happy person. It is not just a deceit that Guido remains happy throughout this story. It is also just who he is. Finally, Guido's energy is a testament to a happier world that really does exist underneath even a concentration camp. This happier world is the one ruled by God, which Scripture refers to as heaven. One of the biggest questions that will arise for us as we move through this unit is the question of what heaven is. Jesus refers to heaven again and again in the Beatitudes. For now, let us just notice an important claim that I have made: that heaven is a deeper reality than a concentration camp. Inside this claim happiness is also an activity of trust for Guido. Just as Joshua trusts in Guido, Guido trusts in heaven.

Let us move more deliberately into the realm of ethics. Is Guido an ethical person? Is Joshua? I believe that they both are. Guido and Joshua are moral people because they imagine a world in which things are as they should be and they actively pursue that world. Both Joshua and Guido live as if heaven were already here. They have a view of their world, a story that they are telling themselves, and it is that story which in this extreme case allows Joshua to survive. I believe that this is exactly what Jesus proclaims in the Beatitudes at the beginning of the Sermon on the Mount. Here are the Beatitudes as they are found in Matthew 5:3–12:

> Happy are the poor in spirit, for theirs is the kingdom of heaven.
>
> Happy are those who mourn, for they will be comforted.
>
> Happy are the meek, for they will inherit the earth.
>
> Happy are those who hunger and thirst for righteousness, for they will be filled.
>
> Happy are the merciful, for they will receive mercy.
>
> Happy are the pure in heart, for they will see God.
>
> Happy are the peacemakers, for they will be called children of God.
>
> Happy are those who are persecuted for righteousness' sake, for theirs is the kingdom of heaven.
>
> Happy are you when people revile you and persecute you and utter all kinds of evil against you falsely on my account. Rejoice and be glad, for your reward is great in heaven, for in the same way they persecuted the prophets who were before you.

At first glance it seems like Jesus is up to exactly the same kind of deception that Guido perpetrates in *Life Is Beautiful*. Jesus takes many of the hardest aspects of human life and says that the people who experience life in this way are happy. Is this intellectually or ethically dishonest? Is Jesus selling us a world in which we should be happy when we mourn, when we are poor, when people revile us and persecute us and utter all kinds of evil against us? If so, then we should want nothing to do with this world. Mourning, poverty, and persecution are not reasons to be happy. Anyone, even Jesus, who tells us something different is wrong. We know this because we know that Jesus again and again shows that he cares deeply for the mourning, the poor, and the persecuted. I believe that, instead of tricking us or expecting something impossible from us, that Jesus is revealing for us the way that the world really is at its core. Again, God's reality (much like Guido's) is much better and much happier than the world we see around us.

A biblical worldview is a view of heaven. Being ethical inside a biblical worldview is acting as if heaven is already here. We expect this to be very difficult, and it is. This is due to the fact that we do not know exactly what heaven looks like. It is, therefore, very hard to live our lives as if heaven is already here, but if we look back to the story of Guido, we do get some guidance about this first basic point.

Living as if heaven is already here is as hard as being happy in a concentration camp. If we imagine ourselves in Guido or Joshua's place, we may even think that it is irresponsible to expect happiness in that kind of situation. We will want to spend more time reflecting together on what is psychologically, materially, and ethically responsible (and by this I mean what is responsible for ourselves in terms of our mental health, in terms of our bodily health, and in terms of the health of our actions) as we learn about heaven and happiness together. For now, let's again recognize another claim that I have made. The shape of what heaven is really like should have an impact on our actions now. That is, what we really expect ourselves to do in difficult situations that really matter is connected to broader ideas of what is good for minds, bodies, and actions. Let me summarize this discussion in the simplest way that I can. Heaven is the deepest reality that there is. Our imagination of what heaven is like should shape our actions in the here and now.

When we look back over these Beatitudes we see that they have much to do with a picture of heaven. They don't paint the picture in the same way that the author of Revelation does (although I would argue that they are not in fundamental conflict either), but a picture of heaven emerges nonetheless. In the chapters that follow in this book I want to move through these Beatitudes one by one and flesh out this picture in a larger story. I will do this by interweaving important lessons from the story of the development of Christian ethics with individual Beatitudes. I hope that by doing this we will be able to learn together both the salient features of ethics in a biblical worldview as well as have a sense of the story of how Christians have tried to lead happy lives.

Happiness

Careful readers will have noticed that in the listing of the Beatitudes above, "Happy" is used rather than "Blessed." The Greek word, *makarios*, which is the word that Matthew used, can be translated to mean either blessed or happy, but most Bibles use "blessed" because Jesus would have been referring to a state of being rather than a subjective emotion. We have already seen an example of happiness as a state of being in Guido's character, a person who is constitutionally happy. In my translation, I am choosing "happy" rather than "blessed" because it adds contrast to the Beatitudes. And it is a traditional goal of the ethical life according to many thinkers throughout the ages. When we think of the Beatitudes in terms of the happiness that they promote, we are thinking about ethics.

At least since Socrates, who lived 400 years before Jesus, one of the main goals of ethics has been happiness. How can people lead a good life? How can people be happy? These are some of the most basic questions in ethics. For this reason it makes sense to structure our learning about ethics around happiness, but since we are interested in ethics in a biblical worldview, it makes sense that we would want to let Jesus define what happiness is. The Beatitudes do this and that is why I have structured these chapters around them.

There were other beatitudes before (and after) Jesus in both Jewish and Greek culture. We can learn more about how Jesus used the structure of the beatitude if we pay some attention to the different meanings that the Greek word *makarios* held in the different cultures in which it was used. In ancient Greek times, a thousand years before Matthew, *makarios* referred to the gods. The blessed ones were the gods. In the Greek usage of Matthew's time, *makarios* came to refer to the elite, the upper crust of society, the wealthy people. We have some of this meaning in our time as well. We sometimes think of movie stars, or professional athletes, or other celebrities, as blessed. *Makarios* was also used in the Greek translation of the Old Testament. There it referred to the results of right living or righteousness. Jesus uses this word in a totally different way. It is not the elite who are blessed. It is not the rich and powerful who are blessed. It is not even the righteous, necessarily. Rather, Jesus pronounces God's blessings on the lowly: the poor, the hungry, the thirsty, the meek, the mourning. When Jesus blesses these people, what is he trying to do? What does it mean to tell someone who is mourning that they will be comforted? Jesus' Beatitudes function in at least three ways: ethically, performatively, and indicatively.

The Beatitudes are ethical statements in that they are intended to inspire action. When we hear that the mourning will be comforted, we should seek to comfort the mourning. In this way the Beatitudes include an ethic. The Beatitudes name those people who should be the focus of our actions. If we want to be ethical, Jesus suggests, we should take action for, with, and on the behalf of the poor, the hungry, the thirsty, the meek, and the mourning.

The Beatitudes are performative statements in that they accomplish action in being spoken. When Jesus says that the mourning will be comforted, the mourning themselves may feel comfort from the words. Perhaps a better example, and the one preferred by J. L. Austin, who in *How to Do Things with Words* did important early writing on performative language, are the vows spoken at a wedding. When the bride and groom say to each other, "I do," they accomplish their marriage. The action of marrying is performed by speaking the words. In order for performative language to be successful, three things are necessary. The words must be spoken in the correct context, there must be an audience, and the audience must have uptake; it must understand the words in the right kind of way. If I were to turn to someone on a crowded subway train and say, "I do," I have not married them. At least the correct context and the uptake are missing from this example. If the subway rider is listening to her iPod, audience is missing as well. The Beatitudes have an audience and a context for believing that what Jesus is saying is true. In that a group of people formed around Jesus and around the disciples who were interested in living their lives according to the Beatitudes, we can suppose that an uptake also happened at the Sermon on the Mount.

Besides being ethical and performative, the Beatitudes are also indicative. We can see this most clearly in the first and eighth Beatitudes. They are set in the present rather than the future. Especially here, but across all the Beatitudes, the purpose is to both bring about a new state of affairs that God has proclaimed and to acknowledge that that state of affairs has already been brought about. The Beatitudes are simply descriptive in this way. Those who mourn will be comforted. This is simply true. At points it may be difficult to believe, but we do believe that comforting will happen, and, if we act to make comforting happen, it will happen more surely.

The Beatitudes as Story?

I have made many arguments in this chapter to support the idea that the Bible is a story and that we need to learn to think in stories if we want to inhabit a biblical worldview. There may be, however, one question or loose end remaining, for Jesus is not telling us a story in the Beatitudes, is he? These are short, performative statements. This is not a story with a beginning, middle, and end. The Beatitudes are curious in that they are, in important ways, simply the end of the story. When Jesus says, "Happy are those who mourn, for they shall be comforted," he is saying that one should make this happen, that it is happening in his saying it, and that it simply will happen. However, unlike Guido from *Life Is Beautiful*, Jesus is not telling a story about happiness, mourning, or comfort.

In fact, you may be wondering why I have chosen to structure a book about ethics that argues for stories on a set of aphorisms when Jesus used so many wonderful parables to tell his gospel and when I have access to not one but four stories (Gospels) about Jesus. There are some good formal reasons for choosing the Beatitudes to talk about ethics and one that I'll be focused on throughout this book is the gift structure of the Beatitudes. Each Beatitude offers a different gift. Gifts are important to both Jewish and Christian moral and religious identities. You'll remember that Jesus commands the cleansed leper to give the gift that Moses had commanded. Gifts always elicit and contain their own stories. Furthermore, the Beatitudes on their own may be more story-like than I am indicating here.

What if we think that people in the crowd would have been mourning? If that is the case, then Jesus would have been telling them their story. It is most likely the case that Jesus was preaching to people who were on the fringes of society. They would have heard his words as if Jesus was speaking to them. Jesus was speaking to them. Jesus' statements in the Beatitudes are all about the concrete realities of real particular people's lives.

It is also the case that Jesus' preaching is part of a larger story that Matthew is telling in his Gospel. Matthew does not simply give us the Sermon on the Mount as a set of good rules or a goal to aim towards (although it has elements of both of these things) but puts the sermon inside the story of Jesus' adventures in Galilee.

TWO

Decisions

Giving Our Life to the Glory of God

> "Happy are the meek,
> for they will inherit the earth."
>
> MATTHEW 5:5

A college friend of mine had a bumper sticker on his car that always made me laugh. To this day I'm not exactly sure why I laughed. I think the bumper sticker was one of those things in life that is both funny ha-ha and funny strange at the same time. It read, "The meek are getting ready." I deeply appreciate humor that assumes a bit of prior knowledge, and the bumper sticker is much funnier if you know the Beatitude about meekness. That's probably why I would laugh funny ha-ha laughter. Still, I was always slightly confused when I saw the bumper sticker, too. I do not know if I understand exactly what it means to be meek, but it seems to me that being humble and calm and patient are all necessary characteristics.

The characteristics that the actor Michael Cera sometimes portrays are probably good examples when it comes to imagining meekness. His characters in both *Juno* and *Nick and Norah's Infinite*

Playlist are pretty meek. In *Juno* especially his character remains supportive and interested, but not to the point of being clingy. In *Nick and Norah's Infinite Playlist* both the characters of Nick and Norah are particularly meek at the end of the movie. After searching all night to find out where their favorite band, the secretive Where's Fluffy?, is playing, they realize that if they stay to watch the concert they will make several of their friends angry. They choose to leave knowing that, while their friends can choose to be jerks, they can choose to diffuse the situation on their own.

Anyway, my friend's bumper sticker still does not seem to me like anything that a Michael Cera character would put on his car. It seems to me that the meek, by definition, would never be getting ready. As soon as the meek started to get ready (to inherit the earth), they would no longer be meek. They would have stopped being patient, humble, and calm. Meekness is something that we can probably best observe in others or that others can best observe in us. We can seek to be more meek, but meekness is likely not something that we can achieve. That's not because it is difficult. It seems to me that being meek is often actually very easy, but meekness is not a possession. As soon as we recognize that we are meek, we become a little less meek. Jesus suggests in this Beatitude that the meek will be given the most significant material gift. They will inherit the earth. Those people who do not seek any kind of worldly power will, in the vision of Jesus' Beatitudes, be given it as an inheritance.

This brings us to an important question. What does meekness have to do with ethics? This is not an easy question to answer, but I want to work at trying to answer it in this chapter. The problem with this question is that meekness is a character trait, something that is true about persons in terms of who they are or perhaps are trying to be. Meekness is not particularly easy to choose.

In this chapter I suggest that ethics is also a question of knowing who we are rather than trying to make the right kinds of decisions based on the right kind of information. This is a somewhat counterintuitive claim, but by the end of the chapter I will endeavor to show you both a good argument for why it is true and what it means for people who are not meek.

Making Decisions

When most people in contemporary society think about ethics, they think about making difficult decisions in the right way. To be sure, ethics is knowing the right thing to do in simple situations as well, but most of us, most of the time, think that the really hard work of ethics is about applying the best information that we can to resolving the really hard decisions that we encounter.

Let me give some examples. There are two kinds of simple decisions that make sense to describe as being ethical. The first are basic decisions that we make all the time, and spend very little effort making. Should I hold the door open for the elderly person? (Of course!) Should I stop to comfort the child who has skinned her knee? (Of course!) Some people may want to argue that these kind of decisions or actions do not rise to the level of being considered ethical; however, many of us would agree that the person that ignores these examples of simple kindnesses is mean in a way that deserves judgement. The other simple decision is the kind that managers at companies like BP and Enron did *not* make before the calamities that their actions produced. It is not ethical to cut corners in favor of profit. It is not ethical to record numbers in accounting records that do not accurately reflect the real value of an investment. Very few of us would want to say that the fraud Enron engaged in leading up to its bankruptcy in 2001 or the short-sightedness leading up to the Deepwater Horizon oil spill in 2010 were simply the costs of doing business. If these disasters had not happened, the profits these unethical projects would have generated would not somehow be okay. These examples should teach us two things. Unethical behavior happens all the time, done by people who should avoid it. The evaluation about whether or not this kind of behavior is unethical is not difficult. It is simply unethical.

One reason that I believe that rules are not as good an approach to ethics as stories is that many of the rules that we would want to create are ones that ordinary people with good sense already know to obey. Speed limits are a really good example of this kind of rule. In Michigan, where I live, the speed limit is seventy miles per hour. Given the conditions of the roads, the size of the engine, shock absorption, and handling of my Honda Civic, the speed of other cars on the roads, and my reaction time, seventy miles per hour is the speed that I am comfortable driving anyway. If I drove twenty miles per hour faster (or slower), I would feel like I was endangering both myself and others. It would not be responsible for me to drive at a significantly different speed. Once a week I drive from Michigan to Ohio. Somewhere around Toledo the speed limit changes from seventy miles per hour to sixty-five miles per hour; however, my speed rarely changes and traffic generally does not start going faster or slower. Almost everyone seems to take the same approach to the rule; they drive safely regardless of the speed limit. When someone, usually someone in a red sports car or some kind of Lexus (I don't know why Lexus drivers seem so much less responsible than other drivers), zips by me at ninety miles per hour, I don't get angry with them for breaking the rule. I am frustrated that they have, in a small way, endangered my life and the lives of those around me. The point here is that the rule describes something that responsible people all already know.

Ethics is not the domain of easy decisions, such as rules we know we should obey, social mores we know we should follow, or egregious acts that no one should ever consider. Ethics is, instead, we often think, the task of making hard decisions in difficult situations. The classic examples are stealing a loaf of bread in order to feed your family or killing an intruder in your home. For a variety of reasons I believe that these two examples are actually easy decisions masquerading as difficult ones, but there will be more on this in later chapters. We can think of difficult situations that we all face every day that we should worry about.

Where should I buy my clothing? At Walmart, where it is cheapest for me, but where third world sweatshops supply the products and most employees with children have historically lived under the poverty line? At a resale shop, where my purchases do not contribute to the economy? At American Apparel, where I can buy sweatshop-free, organic clothing made in the USA, but at expensive prices? Should I eat meat? Donate my used clothing to Goodwill? Rip a CD for a friend? A friend's friend? That annoying guy in my class who won't stop asking? Should I invest my money in the stock market? Keep active a checking account at Chase? None of these questions have easy answers. I think that often we are tempted to think that if we could just get enough good information about these questions, then we could make the right decision.

What about broader life questions? Is choosing a life partner an ethical question? A church? If a woman finds herself pregnant, should she consider an abortion? If my best friend finds herself pregnant, what is my responsibility to her? If my best friend finds himself a potential father, what are my responsibilities to him? If he has decided that it's not his concern, do my responsibilities to him increase or decrease? These questions, as Rowan Williams suggests in a brilliant essay called "Making Moral Decisions," focus our attention on how deeply our relationships with others shape our decision making.

> Think about these and choices like them. Each of them [even ripping a CD for a friend?] is a decision that is colored by the sort of person I am; the choice is not made by a will operating in the abstract, but by someone who is used to thinking and imagining in a certain way: someone who is the sort of person who finds an issue like this an issue of concern.

The Human Person

There are three important claims in this brief quotation. Williams first argues that decisions are "colored" by the sort of people that we are. This claim, which is in keeping with the emphasis on stories that I have been putting forth, is easily supported by example. Just as we can start to predict what a character in a story might do, we can know what we might do in some difficult situations. I know that I am a very patient person. Typically, situations in which other people might become very anxious are not problems for me. This means that crises that arise in the lives of those around me can sometimes benefit by my cooler approach. (I am not saying that I'm better at this than my friends or that being so patient does not also have downsides. I am simply noticing that patient people can sometimes address situations coolly and that we would *expect* them to.)

Along with this connection between a person's character and their decision making, Williams notes that "the choice is not made by a will operating in the abstract." Sometimes we might think that the best way to make a decision is on purely objective grounds. We think that if we did not have any connection we could make a better or even the best decision. John Rawls calls this the *original position*, a purely abstract place that we should seek to inhabit by stripping away all of our personal commitments. Williams is convinced that it is not the case that the best decisions are made in the abstract. Think about how difficult it would be to actually make a decision in the abstract. Let's go back to the example of a friend who is expecting a baby. It is one thing to be convinced that people should be able to choose abortion, or give up children for adoption, or keep their biological offspring. It is another thing to encounter, in the life of someone that you know well, all of the changes that a baby would bring. Williams is arguing that it is foolish to think that we can make decisions outside of the skein of relationships that bind us together.

The final point that Williams makes is that we are people who find certain issues concerning. Perhaps when I was narrating my approach to speeding, you found yourself in total disagreement. Perhaps you are a person who doesn't speed because the law stipulates a maximum speed but, left to your own devices, would happily drive 100 miles per hour all the time. Perhaps you were concerned that I averred such a high ordinary speed and think that fifty miles per hour is a much better speed environmentally, safety wise, and economically. (You are, of course, right that fifty miles an hour is generally a better speed limit on these grounds.) Perhaps you are totally disinterested in speed limits. The point is not any of these particular positions or potential decisions that go with these positions. Williams is noticing that we find one or another issue an issue of concern. Part of what will always make ethics a difficult area is that we are going to have different ideas about what is important ethically. We are colored by the sorts of people we are, we don't make decisions in the abstract, and we find different questions and situations ethically interesting or concerning. In all of these ways the question about what ethics is, in any of its various formulations, is a question about what kind of people we are.

The question about what kind of people we are is an important question for ethics. As we move through these chapters, we will again and again consider different answers to this question. In the next chapter we will consider this question in terms of the constituent parts of the human person (spirit, body, soul). For now, we are interested in terms of the relationships that people are involved in.

Self-Discovery

In the first chapter I argued that we should think about stories if we want to think about ethics in a biblical worldview. In this chapter I have been arguing that ethics is a question about what kind of people we are. I hope that the connection between these two arguments is somewhat easy to make. If I want to think about what kind of person I am, then I do not just think about myself removed from my parents, my hometown, my high school or college, or my friends. I am, in many ways, the person that the main influences in my life have made me. Living in a culture different from the one that you have grown up in is one of the easiest ways to understand this. I grew up in Canada, but now I live in the American Midwest.

As a Canadian I am very apologetic. If you spend some time with Canadians, you will find that generally we are a very apologetic people. We are always apologizing for everything. In fact, in Canada, people regularly apologize back and forth several times as a way of just being polite. Even now, I probably apologize for something or another fifty times a day. If someone were to spill a milkshake on me at lunch I would probably apologize. People in the American Midwest are very nice people, but they do not have this cultural need to apologize for everything. I have felt this at a visceral level ever since I moved here. I would apologize, but the other people would not apologize back. More than anything this made me realize how apologetic I am; however, when I moved from Chicago to northwest Ohio several years ago, I encountered a new cultural saying. People in northwest Ohio like to say "You're fine" whenever anyone apologizes to them. I experience this as a very graceful way to simply close off the apologizing circle. Everyone from Canada should live in northwest Ohio for at least a year.

If ethics is a question about what kind of people we are, then the way that we can best discover what kind of people we are is by discovering ourselves. Part of that work is to reflect on the story of how we came to be where we are now, on the story of our lives; however, we all know that we are not perfect. We know that our parents are not perfect, that people in our hometown are not perfect, and that our churches and nations are not perfect. Ethics cannot be just about who we are, it also needs to be about who we can be if we are our best version of ourselves. In explicitly Christian language we would talk about this as God's plan for our lives. Part of why we are not ethical is that we do not know the plan that God has for us, or worse, we think we do know God's plan but we are wrong about it. I believe that this is one of the biggest obstacles to living a good life.

Herbert McCabe offers an excellent reflection on this obstacle in his book *Law, Love and Language*:

> Ethics is entirely concerned with doing what you want, that is to say with being free. Most of the problems arise from the difficulty of recognising what we want. . . . Remorse differs from regret in just this respect. Regret mean realising that you *now* wish you had not behaved in a certain way; remorse is the realisation that you did not really wish to behave in that way *at the time,* that the behavior was contrary to your deepest desires, your need to be truly yourself. Remorse is much more catastrophic than regret; it is a revolutionary act in the sense that it involves a reassessment of your past, a re-writing of your autobiography.

McCabe is arguing in this quotation that who we are and what we have done is not necessarily who we want to be or what we want to do. When we do something bad, wrong, evil, or unethical, we may regret having done it. This happens when I realize that something that I thought I needed to do at the time turns out to have had very bad consequences. I regret the way in which I ended some of the romantic relationships that I was in during college. I could have been nicer, more forgiving, and more tactful. I wish I could have done that at the time. My deepest desires were and are to be nicer, more forgiving, and more tactful. I failed at that and I regret it. While I wish that I had done better in those situations, I also recognize that breaking up is hard to do and that it is likely the case that I did as well as I could have expected myself to do. I could have done better but that was not for lack of self-knowledge or for lack of trying.

However, I have significant remorse about the way a different particular relationship ended. I did everything I could to stay in that relationship. I became, in a variety of passive-aggressive ways, controlling, needy, and frankly desperate. I remember buying an expensive gift to try and keep this woman interested in me. Some gift. Nothing about it was freely given and everything about it was desperately demanding attention. I was definitely expecting something, anything, in return. In that relationship, I became a person who I now almost do not recognize. In the aftermath of that relationship, I reassessed who I was and worked very diligently to become a different person. I do not recognize who I was then, even though I can remember those situations very clearly, because I have worked to become a different person. In this case I did not fail because I did not try hard enough or because the situation was too difficult for my abilities, but because I acted against what I now know to be my deepest desires.

When I do what I want, what I really want, I am acting in a way that is in accord with my deepest desires, not just for who I am now, but for who I want to be in the future. Notice the ways in which my behavior is performative in this sense. I have knowledge about what I want to do and by doing it I bring that person into being, or, in doing things which I now recognize to be against my deepest desires, I learn about myself and then work from that point. I believe that the Beatitudes are a good guide for ethics partly because they also orient our action towards our deepest desires for the future. The Beatitudes also connect this future, our perfect future, to God's future.

Receiving Gifts

The aspect of the Beatitudes that I want to emphasize at this point is their structure. Let us take the Beatitude about meekness as our example.

> Happy are the meek, for they will inherit the earth (Matt 5:5).

Like all of the eight Beatitudes in Matthew's gospel, this Beatitude follows a very set literary structure. We could analyze this structure in many different ways, but, for now I want us to look at it with the terms that I introduced last chapter: indicative, ethical, and per-formative. Each Beatitude begins with an indicative or descriptive statement that concerns happiness (or blessedness). Each Beatitude describes a group of people as blessed or happy. Each Beatitude then names this group as ethical. Why are they ethical? Following the argument of this chapter, this group is named as ethical because it is something or it does something. This noun is always set in the present tense. This follows with a performative statement; namely that this group of people will receive something. Notice that in every case in Matthew's Beatitudes the performance that happens involves a gift. For this reason I would argue that the Beatitudes have what I would call a "gift structure."

Looking at the Beatitudes this way gives us a better sense of the worldview that Jesus views as the happy life. It is a worldview in which those who are described in the Beatitudes receive gifts. The economy here is an economy of gift. Rather than functioning in an economy of scarcity in which people need to compete for what is important (an economy which creates many of the difficult situa-tions that beg ethical decision making), Jesus suggests that the real economy of God's kingdom is an economy of abundance in which people receive gifts from God.

Rowan Williams is instructive about how this can structure a person's whole life. He says:

> The self that must be discovered is a self already involved very specifically in this kind of community, in relation to

this kind of God [the community and God described in the Beatitudes]. The goal of our decision making is to show what God's selfless attention might mean in prosaic matters of everyday life—but also to show God's glory (look for example, at Romans 15.7 or 1 Corinthians 10.31). What am I to do? I am to act in such a way that my action becomes something given into the live of the community and in such a way that what results is glory—the radiating, the visibility, of God's beauty in the world.

Decisions, for Williams, are opportunities to offer gifts into the community that has formed us so that what results is God's glory. This quotation from Williams is the finest small statement about how to be ethical and happy that I have found. I believe that if we all worked to follow his example, our world and especially our churches would be more moral places and that we would be happier people.

THREE

Gifts

Ethics in an Ancient Hebrew Worldview

"Happy are the poor in spirit,
for theirs is the kingdom of heaven."

MATTHEW 5:3

A t the end of my fourth year of college I injured my back. I spent the first two months of that summer lying on my back, resting, and hoping that my back would recover and that I would not need surgery. At the end of these first two months I was mostly healthy but not healthy enough to try to find a job. I needed some sort of situation where I could keep myself partly busy during the day but could take a break and lie down at a moment's notice if I felt a spasm coming on. I knew the person in charge of Mennonite Volunteer Service, and he suggested that I might be able to go down to Chicago and volunteer for Synapses, a grassroots peace and justice organization. Incidentally, Synapses was the organization that preceded Christian Peacemaker Teams. Anyway, they would probably have some things that I could help with and probably would not mind someone who was lame part of the time.

It is interesting how something like a back injury can change the whole course of your life. It was that summer that I had my first experience of living in the United States, living in a big city, living around poor people, and living around large groups of nonwhite people. It was also the summer that I met the person who became my life partner. Through her I received a fiancé visa and a reason to study in Chicago. Some twenty years later, almost everything about my life still hinges on that summer. Being open to the opportunities that life presents you with is very important to living ethically in a biblical worldview.

However, it would be a mistake to imagine that you need to move away from your hometown or blow out your back or fall in love in order to become ethical. It may be that, as we learned in the last chapter, since many of us think that ethics is about making decisions in difficult situations, we may be more open to thinking about ethics when we are in new situations. This is not because new situations have anything special about them, but because they are new and focus our attention in direct ways; furthermore, new situations are wonderful for teaching us things about ourselves. I learned much about being Canadian, white, and straight when I actually knew people who were not those things.

I also learned much of what I know about poverty that summer. I learned this from two people: Bud Snow and Wayne Forehand. Bud was from the West Side of Chicago where I lived in an home that housed a number of Oblate Mission volunteers. He was poor, but his mother was a community organizer, and so he worked at Synapses doing maintenance work. He was the only paid employee at Synapses, and I think that, because of his circumstances, this was the only job he really had a chance of getting. Wayne, on the other hand, lived in a wealthy part of Chicago and was, I think, quite wealthy himself. It was somewhat interesting to me that he chose to work at a very small organization that was housed in the an old beaten-down house in a bad section of town seeking justice for the poor and oppressed in various locations around the world. I often think of Wayne when I think about the Beatitude in Matthew 5:3.

The phrase "poor in spirit" is a very difficult one to understand. Part of the difficulty is that Matthew reports this Beatitude very different than Luke. Here is the Beatitude from chapter 6 in Luke's gospel:

> Blessed are you who are poor, for yours is the kingdom of God (Luke 6:20).

Note the difference between Luke's "poor" and Matthew's "poor in spirit." Many scholars suggest that Matthew's Beatitudes are spiritual, being concerned with heaven and things of the spirit. In contrast Luke's Beatitudes are seen as being material and being concerned with more concrete realities: our bodies, our earth, whether or not we have enough to eat, and so forth. This argument is strengthened by the fact that Luke includes a series of woes along with his Beatitudes. Luke records Jesus as pronouncing blessing on the poor and woe to the rich:

> But woe to you who are rich, for you have received your consolation (Luke 6:24).

Since Matthew says "poor in spirit" rather than "poor" and since Luke pronounces woe to the rich as well as blessing to the poor, which both sharpens the meaning of poor in Luke's Beatitudes and makes sure that the rich get the point that this is not a blessing for them, scholars have seen Matthew as offering a softer message than Luke. Throughout the Bible, with few exceptions, caring for the poor is seen as holy, righteous, good work. Especially in the Gospels and Pauline letters, the dangers of wealth are very prominent. Matthew could be hedging his message a bit so as to not alienate the wealthy. Matthew could even be suggesting that it is our spirit that matters and not our material situation.

As regards these different renderings of the Beatitudes, Bud would be probably more happy with Luke, and Wayne with Matthew. This kind of reading of Scripture, however, in which we pick and choose the parts of it that make most sense to us, while inevitable in some ways given Scripture's length, breadth, and depth, should jump out at us as a very dangerous way to read the Bible.

Actually, when I read Matthew's Beatitude about the poor in spirit I often think of Wayne. I think about him because, although he did not despise his wealth, he threw in his lot with the poor. No one could call Wayne poor, but he was poor in spirit. It makes sense to me to think about this Beatitude as calling all of us to become poor in spirit by caring for and thinking with and putting ourselves alongside the poor. There is a very strong ethical message here. The blessings in Matthew's and Luke's Beatitudes are first for the concrete, materially poor people. In Matthew, they can be for the rich, but only if the wealthy put their spirits, and by extension their material resources, alongside the poor.

The Human Person

Something else trips us up in thinking about this Beatitude. What does spirit mean? Where is your spirit? Is it in your brain? Your heart? Your pancreas? Your pineal gland? Is having a spirit the same as having a soul? Do you even have a spirit or soul? How does it interact with your body? What is your body, for that matter? We can call these questions ontological questions. Ontological questions are about the essential being of something. There are a set of related questions that it makes sense to also ask now that we are on a roll. What makes me different from you? My faith? My ethnicity? My gender? My hometown? What is more important, the individual or the group? These questions are basically sociological questions, questions about how I fit into my society. When Jesus says that the poor in spirit are blessed because theirs is the kingdom of heaven, does that mean that only our spirits go to heaven? Why does Jesus use a social or group metaphor and not an individual one? People have been asking and answering these question in many different ways for thousands of years.

One of the most popular contemporary ideas about the human person holds that we are really only our bodies and that we do not need to think about any soul or spirit beyond the body. Ideas that people have about religion, God, and something beyond physical reality can all be explained by thinking about the various processes in which our brain engages. Versions of these ideas are particular popular in New Atheism. In contrast to this, many American Christians believe that our bodies are the container for our souls and that after our death only our souls will make the journey to heaven. However, these ideas are both relatively new ones.

The latter idea can be traced back most appropriately to Rene Descartes, a French mathematician and writer. Descartes held that the body was essentially a machine and that it was controlled by the brain and especially by the soul through the mediation of the pineal gland. In this way Descartes' theological anthropology was very dualistic. Soul and body are two different realities, and the only connection is through this small gland. This idea has had a great influence on Western culture and persists in both philosophy and theology, even though it is entirely discredited by advances in biology and neurology. We now know that the pineal gland balances chemicals that help us sleep.

One of the ways that this idea has gained extra authority is by the suggestion of some scholars that the ancient Greek philosophers like Plato and Aristotle also had a dualistic worldview; however, it is probably a mistake to think that Descartes, Plato, and Aristotle thought in similar ways about this. As we will see later, rather than dividing the body and soul, Plato was probably more interested in just despising the body.

Ancient Hebrew Worldview

Any of these ideas would have been very confusing to the Jews that lived hundreds of years before Jesus. Let us refer to these people as the ancient Hebrews. The most important difference would have been regarding the goodness of the body. Descartes does not necessarily think the body is bad, but he thinks of it in the model of a glorious machine that does not value the body as a organic creation of God. Plato does think the body is evil, but in Genesis 1 God creates everything and says that it is good! In very powerful ways the worldview of the ancient Hebrews is one that marvels in the glory of God's created world and delights in its goodness.

People then thought of themselves as belonging first to their society or family. This larger group gave a sense of boundaries, which provided personal identity. Ancient Hebrews had a keen sense of their local environment but remained much more interested in questions of how to be obedient to God's law than in questions of what it meant for them to be individuals. The idea of a self whose inner depths are the warrant or proof of its identity arises in the Western imagination no earlier than Augustine in the fourth century CE and probably only really takes hold by the time of Kant in the eighteenth century CE. Ancient Hebrews looked to God and how God provided for the Jewish people for the warrant or proof of their uniqueness and identity. The group was much more important than the individual.

There was also almost no dualism in ancient Hebrew thought. The only possibility for any dualism was in the separation between two inclinations that where both essential parts of the Hebrew soul. The *yetzer ha ra* (the inclination towards the bad) and the *yetzer ha tov* (the inclination towards the good) are simply attentions to different dimensions of the person in relationship to their creator. Both cut across body and mind and neither is inherently evil. These inclinations signal that in the things we see, feel, and do we can obey God or not. When we follow inclinations that see us obey God's plan for our lives, we choose to connect our lives to God's purpose and, in an ancient Hebrew worldview, this is good. To follow inclinations that go against God's purposes for our lives is bad. To deliberately choose the bad is to commit a genuinely evil act and only the specific choice of the bad, knowing that it is bad, is evil. Simply having an inclination to do bad or good is not.

I think of this this way. Remember, I am generally a very patient person. It is easy for me to extend grace to other people and I often do this. I believe that God's plan for my life (and for people generally) is that they do their best to be nice to each other. There is, however, one area of my life in which I do not have much patience. When I drive I can be very impatient. I think that this has to do with having cars around me drive aggressively too often. People that drive cars too often forget that the other cars on the road are also being driven by people. I have an inclination to drive rudely. I work hard against this, but I do still act on this inclination. Often, however, I do not choose to be rude as a driver. It just happens. The consequences of my actions are still something that I believe I need to bear, but I do not believe that God will hold me accountable for the inclination. Acting like the person that I am is not something that it makes sense to think of as sinful. I have an inclination to good—patience—and an inclination to bad—rude driving. Both of these make me who I am. Neither is evil; however, I have almost no inclination to be rude to people in situations other than driving situations. I need to choose to be rude in these situations, and sometimes I do. I do not know if I think it will be easier or if I want to impress friends (they probably should not be my friends anyway), but I know that I am not as nice as it would be easy for me to be in restaurants or waiting rooms or at church. In these situations when I am being mean for the sake of being mean, I do believe that it is a sin and that I am playing at a game that has long-term consequences that make me sick when I think about them.

It does not make sense for me to describe this as a battle between good and evil raging inside my soul. It makes much more sense for me to notice that I have a personality that responds in relatively predictable ways to many situations. When I act on a bad inclination in the knowledge that I am choosing against God, it is a sin not just against God but against my best knowledge of who I want to be. Even the Hebrew words *basar* (flesh) and *nephesh* (soul) do not provide the opportunity for the separation of the human person into possible component parts. In the *Theological Dictionary of the Old Testament*, N. P. Bratsiotis suggests,

> [W]e are not to think of it as a dualism of soul and body in the Platonic sense. Rather, *basar* and *nephesh* are to be understood as different aspects of man's existence as a twofold entity. It is precisely this emphatic anthropological wholeness that is decisive for the twofold nature of the human being. It excludes any view of a dichotomy between *basar* and *nephesh*, "soul," as irreconcilably opposed to each other, and reveals the mutual organic psychosomatic relationship between them.

This twofold nature is caught well by the many meanings of the word *nephesh*, which, while having a dominant meaning of soul, can also be translated as body or person (the basic meaning is throat or neck). In fact, *nephesh* (soul) does not just apply to humans; it is applicable to animals as well.

The human person in an ancient Hebrew worldview is created good and whole and is fitted with a personality and with character traits that incline them in all sorts of directions. Throughout the Old Testament, the human person is seen as a creature of God created for obedience.

This view of the human person fits into a larger worldview that the ancient Hebrew people had of there world. Of course there is not just one ancient Hebrew worldview just like there is not one American worldview, but the following characteristics are good general first ideas in beginning to understand this way of viewing the world. In a sentence, the ancient Hebrew worldview is focused on gifts and on how God's people receive these gifts.

A Covenant of Gifts

Throughout the Old Testament God makes covenants with God's people. Some of these covenants are, perhaps somewhat surprisingly to us, unconditional. God promises to give God's people order, or never flood the earth again, or present a messiah in the line of David, and they do not need to do anything in return. What does it mean for how we should live our lives that God gives God's people gifts without expecting anything in return?

Unconditional gifts probably make the most amount of sense in context. Many people expect that their mother will always love them no matter what. A mother's love is probably the best example of what "unconditional" means. It is a good example because we expect mothers to love their children. In fact, one of the most jarring plot devices in contemporary cinema is the mother who doesn't love her children. The relationship between a mother and her child is usually characterized by a particularly close relationship that has all kinds of biological reinforcements. These biological reinforcements (changes in hormone levels, etc.) occur for both the mother and the child. They are especially present in the relationships between biological mothers and children; however, it is probably even more interesting to reflect on the fact that they exist even between unrelated persons who occupy these roles relative to one another.

We do not even need to stop at these human examples. The same kinds of biologically reinforced relationship happens between mother and children animals. And, these relationships happen between unrelated animals who act as each other's mothers and children. My favorite example of this is the sea otter Toola who for many years fostered injured or orphaned sea otter pups at the Monterey Bay Aquarium in California. Toola taught her human caretakers that a sea otter could foster a unrelated pup. Before her, humans did not think this could be done. When Toola died in 2012 she was celebrated across the world.

These relationships determine much of what the word *unconditional* has come to mean to us. Each example is entirely dependent on its own story. Note how different, weird, and even potentially problematic it is for me to now pledge my unconditional love to you outside any context other than author and reader. I expect that none of you believe that this pledge is in any way sincere.

When God creates unconditional covenants with God's people, they are done in the context of a particular and strong relationship that God has already established with God's people. The gifts that God gives without expecting anything in return only make sense in terms of a larger economy of gift. Often when we use the word *economy*, we are referring to an exchange. The market economy of capitalism governs the exchange of capital, resources, and wealth in our society. In general, if one party gains in this kind of economy, the other suffers. This type of economy assumes that resources are scarce and that therefore competition is necessary. A gift economy is different. It assumes that resources are abundant, that there is enough, more than enough, for everyone. One of the best examples of a gift economy is forgiveness. There is no limit on how much I can forgive someone, and it does not cost me anything to do it. When God gives gifts to God's people, they are given in this way. Gifts that are given to me are not in competition with gifts given to someone else. In that way the only thing that people need to do with God's gifts is to receive them.

Perhaps some more stories about animals can illustrate this economy of gift. Unconditional relationships even happen across species. You may have read the story of Owen the hippo and Mzee the tortoise, who were brought together after a tsunami in 2004. Or of the inseparable Bobbi the dog and Bob the cat, who survived Hurricane Katrina together, a story all the more remarkable because Bob is blind. My favorite is Aochan the snake and Gohan the hamster, brought together when Aochan decided Gohan would make a better friend than lunch. There are so many examples that these cross-species relationships are now receiving serious scientific study.

It makes sense to think of these relationships as gifted if we remember the connection between gifts and abundance and generosity that oppose the economics of scarcity, insecurity, and fear. Gifts are, however, notoriously difficult for us to give well, to accept, and to understand. If you remember my story about my desperate relationship in college, and even more so if you have had a similar experience, you know what I mean.

Good Gifts

I think we can know three things about the gifts that we give and receive. A good gift happens in the context of a relationship, it is intelligible, and it is appropriate to its relationship. Curiously, the most important thing about gifts is not what is given, but how it is received.

Here's an example of utter failure on my part in receiving a gift. It took me and my wife's parents a few years to figure each other out. One Christmas at their home we were sitting around opening our presents. That year, I had decided that what I really wanted for Christmas was a juicer. I had decided that I should be the kind of person that drank juice—juice made in an expensive juicer. I did not tell anyone that I wanted a juicer because the kind of juicer that I wanted was much more expensive than I was comfortable receiving. So I probably asked for books. I like books too. Anyway, it was finally my turn to open my gift from my wife's parents and, pleasantly, it came in a really big box. I lifted it up and it was really heavy. I opened the paper. Sure enough there on the box it said, in that most beautiful of vaguely Germanic fonts, Braun Multiplex Juicer. I wear my emotions on my sleeve, and my face also just erupted with joy at what I was seeing. My parents-in-law said, "Oh, open the box, Trevor" in a tone I would later understand meant disappointment. I opened the box and what was inside? Stone cat bookends. They had bow ties. This was a very thoughtful gift. As I've said, I like books. My wife and I love cats. And I enjoy art, and these had been handcrafted in Haiti, where my parents-in-law had spent half their lives serving the poor, and working to sustainably develop the countryside. They were, however, not what I wanted, and in the end not the kind of art I most appreciated, and, most disappointingly, that was clear in the expression on my face that Christmas morning.

With that story in our minds let's think together a bit more about the context, intelligibility, and appropriateness of a good gift. Even though I didn't ultimately "like" them, those stone cat bookends were a good gift. They showed that my parents-in-law had thought about me and what they knew I liked and had bought me something appropriate both for our relationship and the occasion. Often the best gifts are given between people who know each other well and can recognize exactly what the other person will like. Sometimes, the best gift is a picture drawn by a child for his mother, or a treasured keepsake given by an old person to her caretaker. Sometimes gifts can become the things that allow us to become who we are. Quality art supplies, a musical instrument, or sports equipment could be examples. Notice with these examples the importance of a relationship in which we might be known better than we know ourselves.

It is also important that a gift be intelligible. If I just walk up to someone during a class that I am teaching and hand them my chalk, have I given an intelligible gift? No. They would probably just look at me, confused. However, notice that a gracious gift receiver could say, "Oh! Some chalk, I have a blackboard in my dorm room and haven't been able to find any chalk to use on it! This is perfect!" This is a good example of the reception of the gift overwhelming the gift itself.

Finally, a gift should be appropriate. Imagine you are asked out on a date. You go, and it's fine. It's not bad, but not really all that good either, just fine. You might try a second date, but you just as easily could be done with it. The next day you open your mailbox and find an expensive piece of jewelry. Is this a good gift? The biggest reason against it is that you are just at the beginning of your relationship with this person and even if it is given with the best of intentions, it is genuinely hard, and potentially dangerous, to receive this gift well. It's not appropriate.

Can we ever give a gift without expecting something in return? We probably cannot answer that questions for ourselves. We probably don't even know if we are expecting something in return. I do believe that we can assert that God can give gifts without expecting anything in return and that is the important point here. In fact, that God does this allows for the possibility that we must be able to, as well. There are four gifts that God gives God's people that model this well.

Creation

The first gift is the gift of creation. God creates a good world. God's people are created good and have a good place to live in, with other good creatures. The story of Adam and Eve tells about this gift. They are created good and have a perfect place in which to live. Only one expectation is placed on them: obedience. They are not to eat from the tree of the knowledge of good and evil. Note that the knowledge of evil is not possible in this mythical perfect state. Evil only enters the story when the people follow an inclination that leads away from God. Obedience is immediately one of the key problems that humans are seen as having in the Old Testament.

Law

So, God gives another gift, the gift of law. Many people assume that when we think of ethics in the Old Testament we should think of the laws. After all, laws give us the rules for how to live our lives. A better way to understand law in a Hebrew worldview is as an answer to the question, "What am I not to do?" The problem with obedience is solved by the law. The gift that the law offers is knowledge about how to avoid acting on bad inclinations. Living by the law is living according to God's will in that the law attempts to protect us from becoming the kind of people that we do not want to become. This emphasis focuses our attention on how the law forms character rather than regulating our lives. Still, the law is not complete as a guide for life, since it is only a negative reinforcement to the good life. The law needs to be understood in the context of God's relationship with God's people.

Election

Therefore, God also gives a third gift that works in tandem with the other two. This is the gift of choosing a people. This gift is the most counterintuitive for our thinking and will require some explanation. One of the scandals of the story of the Hebrew people is that God chooses them instead of choosing some other people or choosing to relate to all of humankind generally. By declaring to Abraham and Sarah that he will establish his covenant with their family, God puts Godself in a particular and strong relationship; however, as we have seen above, it is this relationship that also provides a context for God's unconditional love. We can understand God's unconditional love because God has first loved us.

This gift, the gift of choosing a people, answers the question, "What am I to do?" I am to live like a member of God's community, the people that God has chosen. Taken this way, the gift that is given to the Jewish people overflows the boundaries of that community and is extended to all people. It makes sense in terms of God's relationship to Abraham and Sarah and their descendants, but as a answer to the ethical question "What am I to do?" this gift works for all people who live like the gift is given to them. The salt and light passage in Matthew 5:13–16 suggests that people who live as light to others are doing this work of extending God's gift to all.

Shalom

The goal of these first three gifts is *shalom*. Perhaps most obviously, shalom is a greeting that people in the Middle East use even today. Using shalom as a greeting is similar to saying "peace" to someone when you meet them. Shalom has three deeper shades of meaning. The most common meaning of shalom is material well-being and prosperity. This refers to our physical health, our access to food and care and shelter. Shalom is used this way when in the Bible someone suggests that it would be good to inquire into the shalom of another. In this way shalom refers to a integrated state of well-being or health. The second meaning is focused on justice. This is most connected to our contemporary use of the word *peace*. We often think of peace as the absence of war or of violence. Shalom is better opposed to injustice. Shalom does not just refer to the lack of war but to the restoration or creation of right relationships between individuals or groups. To have shalom means that no persons feel like their concerns are not being heard. Finally, shalom can refer to personal integrity and honesty. These three meanings should not be thought of as options but, instead, should be thought of as shades of meaning that come together to provide a full picture. True shalom involves physical well-being, justice, and integrity. It suggests that everything is exactly as it should be.

However, shalom is very difficult to reach. Shalom suggests not just that everything is right in our lives but that everything is right in everyone's life. True shalom means that we have done everything in our power to stamp out injustice wherever it occurs. Perhaps this a reward that we will only achieve in heaven, but we should not assume that this means that it is any less important to work for it now.

I'm pretty sure that that is what both Bud and Wayne were doing that summer as they worked together to try to bring more peace to the world. And it is what I was trying to do in moving to Chicago. We were all working toward shalom because we were trying to be open to God's gifts, and it is in that openness that we make the first few steps towards becoming ethical people.

FOUR

Paradigms

Learning How to Be Good

"Happy are you when people revile you and persecute you
and utter all kinds of evil against you falsely on my account.
Rejoice and be glad, for your reward is great in heaven,
for in the same way they persecuted the prophets
who were before you."

MATTHEW 5:11–12

One of my strongest memories of learning how to be the person that I am happened to me in school. The classroom was an old room on the second floor of an old house that the theology department at Loyola University Chicago used for overflow offices and graduate classes. This old house, called Stebler Hall, sat uncomfortably on one edge of campus surrounded by big institutional buildings. The grass never grew very well, because there wasn't enough sun or too many people walked on the ground. The professor came into class, set down his books, and then said something close to, "Stay here but watch me." He left the classroom and started moving quickly downstairs. He passed out of view. We all did the only thing that would could do in terms of watching. We moved to the window. Sure enough, he appeared in our view, looked up briefly to make sure we could see him, and then knelt down in the ground and ran his fingers through the earth. Immediately, I understood that he was teaching us how important it was to actually do the things that we read about in our course texts. We were reading something for that day about how we needed to run our hands through the earth to feel its pull on us; it might have been a poem by Pablo Neruda. I know that this professor loved poetry. The memory is strong for me not because I learned the material particularly well. I do not remember the author or the quotation, although I am confident that I did learn the idea through my professor's performance. The memory is strong for me because I learned a good deal that day about how I liked to be taught and about how I teach. I found the concrete example very useful. I enjoyed the way I was made to search for knowledge by getting up out of my chair and going over to the window. I also really appreciated having an opportunity to learn in this sideways way. When I talked to my classmates later about how class was begun that day, I found that not everyone agreed. Some thought it was too much of a stunt. Others thought it was a waste of valuable time.

I share this story here because it is one of my favorite stories about how I have been able to learn by example. When I now reflect on the kind of teacher that I have become, I can recognize that I was learning about how to teach even when I thought I was learning about social theory. An important part of this story is both the fact that I learned from this professor and that I recognized that that was the kind of teacher that I would like to be. This professor was a good example for me (although probably not for others) because I could recognize myself in what he was doing. I rarely do things like digging my hands in the earth as a part of class, partly because I do not read much poetry and partly because I have a very different personality than this professor. But I have always admired anyone who can take a difficult or important idea and make it simple or practical. I try to do this, and, when I do it well, I think, "Yes, that was done in the same way as the professor who was before you."

The Beatitude in Matthew 5:11–12 breaks structure with the other eight, so much so that scholars wonder whether or not to count it as a separate Beatitude. It is very similar to the Beatitude that precedes it. The particular difference comes in Jesus' insistence that the people who are being persecuted for his sake are like the prophets of old, who were also persecuted. Their persecution, and subsequent reward, makes sense because the persecuted find themselves imitating the prophets. Prophets in the Old Testament are people who speak for God; likewise, Jesus blesses the persecuted because they endure persecution on his account. The persecuted are persecuted because they have given witness, either spoken or lived, to Jesus. In this way the prophets are examples for all of Jesus' followers, both in terms of how to live their lives and for what to expect when they are doing it right.

Learning from Example

Learning happens best when we can observe in others what it is that we should do. There are some obvious examples of this. If I want to learn how to use a hammer, it is a bad idea for me to read a manual. Someone may be able to give me some helpful hints, but what I need to do in order to use the hammer effectively is watch someone do it and then work at doing it myself. It is certainly also the case that when I use a hammer I need to pay attention to the hammer in the right kind of way. If I am too directly focused on holding the hammer just so and hitting the nail right in the center of the hammer, I will likely only hit my thumb. This is the difference between focused (or direct) and diffused (or indirect) awareness. The use of the hammer requires a good deal of diffused awareness rather than just focused awareness. My attention needs to be diffused or spread out on the different aspects of hammering generally, rather than focused in on each aspect of the task.

I need to let the hammer become like an extension of my hand or probably more accurately, my arm. I need to use the hammer in the same way as the person showing me does it, but my arm needs to learn this more than my brain. We call this kind of knowledge muscle memory. It is something that musicians, actors, and athletes typically learn about as part of their training.

This lesson is a difficult one for me personally, since many of the things that I have tried to learn from others that involve this kind of imitation I find really difficult to learn. I am much stronger at focal than subsidiary awareness and have more difficulty training my muscles to do things than many other people that I know. There is really only one area in which I think that I understand what diffused awareness and muscle memory mean and that is playing Ultimate Frisbee. The experience of running, jumping, extending, and catching a Frisbee that I suspect I cannot catch is one of realizing that my hands, arms, legs, and feet are capable beyond the places I imagine they can be.

Paradigms

Some of the best examples of this type of learning and memory are in the field of professional athletics. Hayley Wickenheiser, Michael Jordan, Serena Williams, Tiger Woods, Mia Hamm, and Wayne Gretzky were so good at their respective sports that they can be said to have transformed their sports in important ways. Even though the play of any of these athletes is creative and original, they all owe their success to the players who played before them, and any of them will acknowledge the greats in talking about their own play. These players are special, though.

They have become so good at their sport that they change what it means to play that sport. For example, Serena Williams and her sister Venus introduced an element of power to the sport of women's tennis that a whole new group of players have needed to imitate in order to be effective. Wayne Gretzky, the great Canadian hockey player, tried to maintain possession of the puck behind his opponents' goal, giving him a virtual one-person advantage every time he was on the ice. Tiger Woods does not play the game differently than his competitors, but is simply so practiced that he always wins. Well, he always won until he let circumstances in his life get so out of control that his practice and concentration were affected.

Michael Jordan dominated the sport of basketball over a long period of time partly because he was capable of great feats of offensive and defensive dominance, but also because he played with exactly the right other players in people like Scottie Pippen, John Paxson, and Steve Kerr. It is Jordan that we remember because when the time came to make the play count, Jordan would come through. He was clutch. He was the paradigmatic basketball player. Even if you do not know the word *paradigmatic*, you could probably recognize that Wickenheiser, Jordan, Williams, Woods, Hamm, and Gretzky are all paradigmatic. They represent, perhaps even to the point of transcending, the standard for their sport. Paradigmatic figures loom large in our imagination. You could probably name the paradigmatic cellist even if you never listen to cello music.

Derived from the Greek, *paradigm* means "a pattern or model or an outstandingly clear or typical example." The word *paradigm* took on a new meaning in the 1960s thanks to the work of the scientist Thomas Kuhn. In his *The Structure of Scientific Revolutions* he suggested that paradigm applies to the normal state of affairs in science. He went on to argue that paradigms can be shifted so that the normal state of affairs can be shifted to reflect a "new" normal. This process is a *paradigm shift*. Waldemar Janzen's *Old Testament Ethics: A Paradigmatic Approach* uses this idea of a paradigm to talk about the way that the stories in the Old Testament provided guidance through paradigmatic figure like Abraham. Here is how he describes a paradigm:

> [B]iblical Israelites did not carry with them a stock of maxims or principles, but mental images of model persons. Such inner images had wholeness and embodied the rich and multifaceted qualities of exemplary behavior appropriate to a given sphere of life. In other words, before the Israelites' inner eye stood a vivid lifelike yet ideal family member, worshiper, wise person, king or prophet. The familial ideal or paradigm was not Abraham, but the figure of Abraham contributed certain aspects to that paradigm through stories such as Genesis 13. . . . Instead, it was a composite image shaped from aspects of the stories of all these and others. Such a personal paradigm is not created by abstracting a principle from a story like Genesis 13 and

> then reclothing it with lifelike features. On the contrary,
> ethical model stories flow together directly to form such
> a paradigm before the mental eye, as the pieces of a jigsaw
> puzzle fit together to yield a picture.

Janzen here suggests that paradigms are "mental images of model persons . . . of exemplary behavior appropriate to a given sphere of life." Just as I should look at Michael Jordan if I want to learn about exemplary basketball playing, other people represent given spheres of life in exemplary ways. It is important to note that I do not necessarily look at one person to model every aspect of my life. Instead, if I want to be patient I should find a patient person from which to learn. If I want to be kind, I should look at the life of a kind person and pay attention to how she finds opportunities to be kind to others and to herself in everyday life. These can be people close to me that I can actually observe, as in the hammer example, but I could also listen to stories of patient or kind people. Our approach to the Old Testament as a source of ethical model stories follows this approach. Finally, in learning from different examples of different paradigmatic figures, we need to integrate our learnings in a composite paradigm of the good life. No one person will give us everything we need. Instead, we need to learn both who to pay attention to and what about them is worthy of my attention. We can learn a great deal from Tiger Woods about how to play golf. We can learn much less from him about how to be married. Paying attention to this difference is the difficult work of ethics, and this work is always going to be highly dependent on the details of the story.

Paradigmatic Stories

In his book, Janzen goes through four model stories, one for each of the four offices of the Hebrew people after the time of the judges. These four offices were basically the different leadership positions in ancient Israel: priest, prophet, sage, and king. A priest is someone who is holy and zealous for God. A prophet is someone who speaks for God and on rare occasions offers God's forgiveness. A sage is someone gifted with common sense and able to reduce conflict and see through difficult situations to beneficial solutions. A king is someone who is able to lead with the best interests of the people and of God at heart.

Janzen looks at stories from Numbers 25, 1 Samuel 24 and 25, and 1 Kings 21. In the rest of this chapter let's work together through these stories to discover their paradigmatic significance. I can't overestimate the importance of reading through them. They follow here for your convenience, but there are great advantages to getting out your Bible and reading them there. In each case I'll give some background and other notes.

I also have a set of questions to think about as you are reading through these stories. These questions are designed to help you read, or better, to help you pay attention.

What happens in the story? What is the main action? You could even think about describing the story in terms of the gift structure I introduced earlier to study the Beatitudes generally and which I'll flesh out a bit here; what is described, what ethical actions are called for or enacted, and what performances are happening or what new relationships are brought into being?

Who are the main characters in the story? Do some seem good, or bad? Do they do particularly good, or bad, or memorable things? Does the story seem to value their action? If you needed to choose one as the paradigmatically good character in the story, who would it be?

Based on the descriptions above, what ancient Israelite office does your paradigmatically good character represent? Is she a paradigmatic sage or priest? Is he a paradigmatic king or prophet? Why is this character worthy of our attention? Are there clues in the story that suggest this to you? Does the paradigmatic character transform his or her office in similar ways to the way that Gretzky transformed hockey or Williams transformed tennis? Are they able to embody their roles in a special way?

Grand Theft Deity: A Story about Sex, Violence, and Worship Allegiance

The problem in this story, from the perspective of the author of Numbers, is that Israel as a nation is supposed to keep themselves racially and religiously pure. Instead they start to have sex with the Moabites. This is a big problem both because the Israelites are mixing with the Moabites and because worship of Baal, the Moabite god, is performed by having sex. Baal is the lead god in the Moabite fertility cult and the way to worship Baal is to perform acts of fertility in order to guarantee the fertility of your farming efforts. The tent of meeting is the main place where the people of Israel worship the LORD.

> While Israel was staying at Shittim, the people began to have sexual relations with the women of Moab. These invited the people to the sacrifices of their gods, and the people ate and bowed down to their gods. Thus Israel yoked itself to the Baal of Peor, and the LORD's anger was kindled against Israel. The LORD said to Moses, "Take all the chiefs of the people, and impale them in the sun before the LORD, in order that the fierce anger of the LORD may turn away from Israel." And Moses said to the judges of Israel, "Each of you shall kill any of your people who have yoked themselves to the Baal of Peor."
>
> Just then one of the Israelites came and brought a Midianite woman into his family, in the sight of Moses and in the sight of the whole congregation of the Israelites, while they were weeping at the entrance of the tent of meeting. When Phinehas son of Eleazar, son of Aaron the priest, saw it, he got up and left the congregation. Taking a spear in his hand, he went after the Israelite man into the tent, and pierced the two of them, the Israelite and the woman, through the belly. So the plague was stopped among the people of Israel. Nevertheless those that died by the plague were twenty-four thousand.
>
> The LORD spoke to Moses, saying: "Phinehas son of Eleazar, son of Aaron the priest, has turned back my wrath from the Israelites by manifesting such zeal among them on my behalf that in my jealousy I did not consume the

Israelites. Therefore say, 'I hereby grant him my covenant of peace. It shall be for him and for his descendants after him a covenant of perpetual priesthood, because he was zealous for his God, and made atonement for the Israelites.'"

The name of the slain Israelite man, who was killed with the Midianite woman, was Zimri son of Salu, head of an ancestral house belonging to the Simeonites. The name of the Midianite woman who was killed was Cozbi daughter of Zur, who was the head of a clan, an ancestral house in Midian. (Numbers 25)

The Nonviolent Godfather (Well, in This Case Anyway)

Saul was the first king of Israel. After awhile God became displeased with Saul's leadership and suggested that the priest Samuel look for a new king. You can read about this story in 1 Samuel 16. Saul was displeased with David and sought him to kill him. We join the story just after David has experienced a narrow escape from Saul, which included Saul being diverted to go and fight the Philistines.

When Saul returned from following the Philistines, he was told, "David is in the wilderness of En-gedi." Then Saul took three thousand chosen men out of all Israel, and went to look for David and his men in the direction of the Rocks of the Wild Goats. He came to the sheepfolds beside the road, where there was a cave; and Saul went in to relieve himself. Now David and his men were sitting in the innermost parts of the cave. The men of David said to him, "Here is the day of which the LORD said to you, 'I will give your enemy into your hand, and you shall do to him as it seems good to you.'" Then David went and stealthily cut off a corner of Saul's cloak. Afterward David was stricken to the heart because he had cut off a corner of Saul's cloak. He said to his men, "The LORD forbid that I should do this thing to my lord, the LORD's anointed, to raise my hand against him; for he is the LORD's anointed." So David scolded his men severely and did not permit them to attack Saul. Then Saul got up and left the cave, and went on his way.

Afterwards David also rose up and went out of the cave and called after Saul, "My lord the king!" When Saul looked behind him, David bowed with his face to the ground, and did obeisance. David said to Saul, "Why do you listen to the words of those who say, 'David seeks to do you harm'? This very day your eyes have seen how the LORD gave you into my hand in the cave; and some urged me to kill you, but I spared you. I said, 'I will not raise my hand against my lord; for he is the LORD's anointed.' See, my father, see the corner of your cloak in my hand; for by the fact that I cut off the corner of your cloak, and did not kill you, you may know for certain that there is no wrong or treason in my hands. I have not sinned against you, though you are hunting me to take my life. May the LORD judge between me and you! May the LORD avenge me on you; but my hand shall not be against you. As the ancient proverb says, 'Out of the wicked comes forth wickedness'; but my hand shall not be against you. Against whom has the king of Israel come out? Whom do you pursue? A dead dog? A single flea? May the LORD therefore be judge, and give sentence between me and you. May he see to it, and plead my cause, and vindicate me against you."

When David had finished speaking these words to Saul, Saul said, "Is this your voice, my son David?" Saul lifted up his voice and wept. He said to David, "You are more righteous than I; for you have repaid me good, whereas I have repaid you evil. Today you have explained how you have dealt well with me, in that you did not kill me when the LORD put me into your hands. For who has ever found an enemy, and sent the enemy safely away? So may the LORD reward you with good for what you have done to me this day. Now I know that you shall surely be king, and that the kingdom of Israel shall be established in your hand. Swear to me therefore by the LORD that you will not cut off my descendants after me, and that you will not wipe out my name from my father's house." So David swore this to Saul. Then Saul went home; but David and his men went up to the stronghold. (1 Sam 24)

The Godfather Part Two: The Foolish Protection Client

This story picks up right where the last one left off. David, now free from Saul's malevolent attention, continues to provide protection for farmers and expects fair payment. Nabal turns out to be a particularly foolish client.

There was a man in Maon, whose property was in Carmel. The man was very rich; he had three thousand sheep and a thousand goats. He was shearing his sheep in Carmel. Now the name of the man was Nabal, and the name of his wife Abigail. The woman was clever and beautiful, but the man was surly and mean; he was a Calebite. David heard in the wilderness that Nabal was shearing his sheep. So David sent ten young men; and David said to the young men, "Go up to Carmel, and go to Nabal, and greet him in my name. Thus you shall salute him: 'Peace be to you, and peace be to your house, and peace be to all that you have. I hear that you have shearers; now your shepherds have been with us, and we did them no harm, and they missed nothing, all the time they were in Carmel. Ask your young men, and they will tell you. Therefore let my young men find favor in your sight; for we have come on a feast day. Please give whatever you have at hand to your servants and to your son David.'"

When David's young men came, they said all this to Nabal in the name of David; and then they waited. But Nabal answered David's servants, "Who is David? Who is the son of Jesse? There are many servants today who are breaking away from their masters. Shall I take my bread and my water and the meat that I have butchered for my shearers, and give it to men who come from I do not know where?" So David's young men turned away, and came back and told him all this. David said to his men, "Every man strap on his sword!" And every one of them strapped on his sword; David also strapped on his sword; and about four hundred men went up after David, while two hundred remained with the baggage.

But one of the young men told Abigail, Nabal's wife, "David sent messengers out of the wilderness to salute our master; and he shouted insults at them. Yet the men were very good to us, and we suffered no harm, and we never missed anything when we were in the fields, as long as we were with them; they were a wall to us both by night and by day, all the while we were with them keeping the sheep. Now therefore know this and consider what you should do; for evil has been decided against our master and against all his house; he is so ill-natured that no one can speak to him."

Then Abigail hurried and took two hundred loaves, two skins of wine, five sheep ready dressed, five measures of parched grain, one hundred clusters of raisins, and two hundred cakes of figs. She loaded them on donkeys and said to her young men, "Go on ahead of me; I am coming after you." But she did not tell her husband Nabal. As she rode on the donkey and came down under cover of the mountain, David and his men came down toward her; and she met them. Now David had said, "Surely it was in vain that I protected all that this fellow has in the wilderness, so that nothing was missed of all that belonged to him; but he has returned me evil for good. God do so to David and more also, if by morning I leave so much as one male of all who belong to him."

When Abigail saw David, she hurried and alighted from the donkey, fell before David on her face, bowing to the ground. She fell at his feet and said, "Upon me alone, my lord, be the guilt; please let your servant speak in your ears, and hear the words of your servant. My lord, do not take seriously this ill-natured fellow, Nabal; for as his name is, so is he; Nabal is his name, and folly is with him; but I, your servant, did not see the young men of my lord, whom you sent.

Now then, my lord, as the LORD lives, and as you yourself live, since the LORD has restrained you from bloodguilt and from taking vengeance with your own hand, now let your enemies and those who seek to do evil to my lord be like Nabal. And now let this present that your servant has brought to my lord be given to the young men who follow my lord. Please forgive the trespass of your servant; for the LORD will certainly make my lord a sure house, because my lord is fighting the battles of the LORD; and evil shall not be found in you so long as you live. If anyone should rise up to pursue you and to seek your life, the life of my lord shall be bound in the bundle of the living under the care of the LORD your God; but the lives of your enemies he shall sling out as from the hollow of a sling. When the LORD has done to my lord according to all the good that he has spoken concerning you, and has appointed you prince over Israel, my lord shall have no cause of grief, or pangs of conscience, for having shed blood without cause or for having saved himself. And when the LORD has dealt well with my lord, then remember your servant."

David said to Abigail, "Blessed be the LORD, the God of Israel, who sent you to meet me today! Blessed be your good sense, and blessed be you, who have kept me today from bloodguilt and from avenging myself by my own hand! For as surely as the LORD the God of Israel lives, who has restrained me from hurting you, unless you had hurried and come to meet me, truly by morning there would not have been left to Nabal so much as one male." Then David received from her hand what she had brought him; he said to her, "Go up to your house in peace; see, I have heeded your voice, and I have granted your petition."

Abigail came to Nabal; he was holding a feast in his house, like the feast of a king. Nabal's heart was merry within him, for he was very drunk; so she told him nothing at all until the morning light. In the morning, when the wine had gone out of Nabal, his wife told him these things, and his heart died within him; he became like a stone. About ten days later the LORD struck Nabal, and he died.

When David heard that Nabal was dead, he said, "Blessed be the LORD who has judged the case of Nabal's insult to me, and has kept back his servant from evil; the LORD has returned the evil-doing of Nabal upon his own head." Then David sent and wooed Abigail, to make her his wife. When David's servants came to Abigail at Carmel, they said to her, "David has sent us to you to take you to him as his wife." She rose and bowed down, with her face to the ground, and said, "Your servant is a slave to wash the feet of the servants of my lord." Abigail got up hurriedly and rode away on a donkey; her five maids attended her. She went after the messengers of David and became his wife. (1 Sam 25:2–42)

Be Careful What You Wish For

Our final story is mostly concerned with the actions of King Ahab of Samaria. It is a classic story of faithfulness, deception, entrapment, and forgiveness. Like a typical king, Ahab wasn't satisfied with governing Israel and all the perks that came with it. Instead he wanted Naboth's vineyard as a vegetable garden, and for some reason became despondent when it didn't work out. Ahab comes to want a variety of things in this story and some are better than others. He talks to a variety of people about these desires and some of these conversations are better than others.

Naboth the Jezreelite had a vineyard in Jezreel, beside the palace of King Ahab of Samaria. And Ahab said to Naboth, "Give me your vineyard, so that I may have it for a vegetable garden, because it is near my house; I will give you a better vineyard for it; or, if it seems good to you, I will give you its value in money." But Naboth said to Ahab, "The LORD forbid that I should give you my ancestral inheritance." Ahab went home resentful and sullen because of what Naboth the Jezreelite had said to him; for he had said, "I will not give you my ancestral inheritance." He lay down on his bed, turned away his face, and would not eat.

His wife Jezebel came to him and said, "Why are you so depressed that you will not eat?" He said to her, "Because I spoke to Naboth the Jezreelite and said to him, 'Give me your vineyard for money; or else, if you prefer, I will give you another vineyard for it'; but he answered, 'I will not give you my vineyard.'" His wife Jezebel said to him, "Do you now govern Israel? Get up, eat some food, and be cheerful; I will give you the vineyard of Naboth the Jezreelite."

So she wrote letters in Ahab's name and sealed them with his seal; she sent the letters to the elders and the nobles who lived with Naboth in his city. She wrote in the letters, "Proclaim a fast, and seat Naboth at the head of the assembly; seat two scoundrels opposite him, and have them bring a charge against him, saying, 'You have cursed God and the king.' Then take him out, and stone him to death." The men of his city, the elders and the nobles who lived in his city, did as Jezebel had sent word to them. Just as it was written in the letters that she had sent to them, they proclaimed a fast and seated Naboth at the head of the assembly. The two scoundrels came in and sat opposite him; and the scoundrels brought a charge against Naboth, in the presence of the people, saying, "Naboth cursed God and the king." So they took him outside the city, and stoned him to death. Then they sent to Jezebel, saying, "Naboth has been stoned; he is dead."

As soon as Jezebel heard that Naboth had been stoned and was dead, Jezebel said to Ahab, "Go, take possession of the vineyard of Naboth the Jezreelite, which he refused to give you for money; for Naboth is not alive, but dead." As soon as Ahab heard that Naboth was dead, Ahab set out to go down to the vineyard of Naboth the Jezreelite, to take possession of it.

Then the word of the LORD came to Elijah the Tishbite, saying: Go down to meet King Ahab of Israel, who rules in Samaria; he is now in the vineyard of Naboth, where he has gone to take possession. You shall say to him, "Thus says the LORD: Have you killed, and also taken possession?" You shall say to him, "Thus says the LORD: In the place where dogs licked up the blood of Naboth, dogs will also lick up your blood."

Ahab said to Elijah, "Have you found me, O my enemy?" He answered, "I have found you. Because you have sold yourself to do what is evil in the sight of the LORD, I will bring disaster on you; I will consume you, and will cut off from Ahab every male, bond or free, in Israel; and I will make your house like the house of Jeroboam son of Nebat, and like the house of Baasha son of Ahijah, because you have provoked me to anger and have caused Israel to sin. Also concerning Jezebel the LORD said, 'The dogs shall eat Jezebel within the bounds of Jezreel.' Anyone belonging to Ahab who dies in the city the dogs shall eat; and anyone of his who dies in the open country the birds of the air shall eat."

(Indeed, there was no one like Ahab, who sold himself to do what was evil in the sight of the LORD, urged on by his wife Jezebel. He acted most abominably in going after idols, as the Amorites had done, whom the LORD drove out before the Israelites.)

> When Ahab heard those words, he tore his clothes and put sackcloth over his bare flesh; he fasted, lay in the sackcloth, and went about dejectedly. Then the word of the LORD came to Elijah the Tishbite: "Have you seen how Ahab has humbled himself before me? Because he has humbled himself before me, I will not bring the disaster in his days; but in his son's days I will bring the disaster on his house." (1 Kgs 21:5–29)

There are a number of things that become clear when we take the time to think our way through stories like these. I think the most significant is that people and the stories they inhabit can be very complex. David is a hero of the biblical story, but he doesn't always act like one. And while these stories have some wonderful tales of repentance, loyalty, and faithfulness, there is also sex, drunkenness, violence, betrayal, and vengeance. The Bible (in both Testaments) is a really interesting book, in every sense of the word *interesting*. Yet a great advantage of a paradigmatic approach is that it allows us to think through the stories and recognize what is truly life giving about them.

The Composite Paradigm

Phineas is not a guy I would like to hang around with; but I do learn about what true commitment to holiness looks like when I think about his story. I actually detest everything about Phineas, including his bloody spear of judgement; but one of the things I love about the Bible is the way that I need to keep checking my own sense of what is good ethics against the stories that the Bible tells me. There may never have been a priest more zealous than Phineas; what does that tell me about how to be holy now, as a pacifist, and as someone who is tolerant of other faiths and sexual practices I don't understand?

David is a model leader in his encounter with Saul. He respects Saul, and especially the office of the king, even though Saul has been trying to kill him. Every word he utters is exactly right in 1 Samuel 24. This makes 1 Samuel 25 all the more surprising. David is well within his rights to expect Nabal to pay him and Nabal is a fool to not respect the future king (Nabal means foolish in Hebrew), but David is by no means accommodating or generous in his treatment of Nabal and his property. David leads well for much of his kingship and it is not surprising that he is the model king in Israel's story, but he is not an unblemished hero. The story of Bathsheba proves that beyond a shadow of a doubt.

Abigail, on the other hand, does seem like she has it all together. She listens to the young man and gives his testimony credibility. That he decided to talk to her at all indicates that she must have had a good reputation both as a reasonable person and as someone who could get things done. She understands that she needs to circumvent her husband and pay David for his protection. She speaks as eloquently to David as he spoke to Saul when the situation was reversed. In fact, that the Saul story is set in the immediate past is another note against David. Why hasn't David learned from his experience? On the other hand, David does recognize immediately that Abigail understood the situation better than anyone. He names her as having good sense and even recognizes that she has prevented his needless bloodguilt. We don't get many Hollywood romances in the Bible, but we get the hint of one at the end of this story.

We have our priest, our king, and our sage, and so we have only one character and office left. Which is good, because we have many strong characters in 1 Kings 21. Jezebel is a strong-willed woman who knows how to get what she wants, or what she wants her husband to want, and she seems capable of doing anything to make it happen. Her husband, King Ahab, certainly redeems himself by the end of the story, humbling himself and begging forgiveness. It's not paradigmatically kingly behavior, but there are things we can learn from his about-face. Naboth is very loyal to his family's heritage and to his land. This is a good thing. Elijah will be our paradigmatic figure, though, as he fulfills the prophetic office of speaking for God. Elijah is an exemplary prophet because he transforms the office of prophet by not simply speaking for God but by also offering God's forgiveness.

Perhaps you chose different characters and placed them in different offices. You were not wrong. In fact, if what I have been saying about performance and Scripture is right then we will recognize that we learn something with each different interpretation. It is when we do the difficult work of putting all of these stories together, looking for the good in each, and building a composite from which we can begin to discern the good in other situations that we will have begun to learn how to be good ourselves.

FIVE

Practices

Working Towards a Goal

"Happy are the pure in heart
for they shall see God."

MATTHEW 5:8

Flow

In an interview in *Wired* magazine the Hungarian psychologist Mihály Csíkszentmihályi proposed that we use the term *flow* to talk about those times when we find ourselves

> completely involved in an activity for its own sake. The ego falls away. Time flies. Every action, movement, and thought follows inevitably from the previous one, like playing jazz. Your whole being is involved, and you're using your skills to the utmost.

When do you experience flow? Playing a sport or a musical instrument? Studying for school? Spending time with your friends? Perhaps, like me, you occasionally experience flow during all of these activities. If you are like me, you also have probably wondered why you do not always experience flow when you do these things. Csíkszentmihályi suggests that flow occurs at the center of a variety of other emotional states. We need to not be too depressed or too anxious, challenged but not frustrated, and inside an area of expertise. All of our attention is focused within a relatively narrow band of activity.

Let me tell a few stories of flow as a way of working towards an understanding of the elements of flow. I think that flow is one of the best ways to understand Matthew 5:8 and also one of the best ways to understand the ethics of the Greek philosopher Aristotle.

I have been lucky enough in my life to play a great deal of Ultimate Frisbee. I started playing Frisbee in Chicago with a group of friends, all of whom were doing some kind of voluntary service in the city. We would descend on Douglas Park at 2:30 on Sunday afternoons, find a few pieces of trash to mark some goals, and then play for a couple of hours. All around us would be people out for a walk or playing soccer or baseball or just lounging their way through Sunday afternoon. We played all year long, year in and year out. I would regularly be amazed by 5:30 that I had just run for three hours. Not only did time stand still when I played Frisbee, but I had more endurance, accuracy, and speed than I would think of myself as having in other contexts. After years of playing with the same people every week, this experience only intensified. When you do the same thing with the same people over and over again, you all get better together in similar ways. I would often be able to throw the Frisbee without looking, just expecting that a friend would have made their usual cut up the field, and sure enough they would catch the disc. The Frisbee that I played in Chicago was totally informal. We did not play with any of the ordinary rules of Ultimate Frisbee. I have the very interesting experience now, when I play with people who have played league Frisbee, of not knowing anything about where I am "supposed" to be on the field but having really good fundamental skills. I seem simultaneously gifted and clueless.

The first fall that I moved out to Winnipeg for Bible college, I fell into a group of people that loved to play music together. There was not a surplus of keyboard players, so I had lots of opportunities to jam with these new friends. Playing music together with friends is another flow activity for me. After a couple of months some of my friends from back home traveled out to Winnipeg to visit me and other common friends. I invited them to join us at a jam session, and we were able to introduce a couple of our songs from back home and play them for the Winnipeg people. After practice, my old friends came up to me and wondered how I was able to play the keyboard so much better in just a couple of months, especially on songs that we had worked on together but that I had not played since leaving home. I had no idea that my playing had changed, and I am still not sure that I became that much better a musician or improviser in that time; however, I know that being around different people with different musical tastes really did expand my own horizon of what was possible as a keyboard player.

To finish my doctorate in theology I needed to write a major paper under the direction of a professor at my graduate school. I would receive direction in occasional meetings after having sent thirty to fifty pages of text to my director a couple of weeks ahead of time. I would show up at his office at around ten in the morning with a big cup of coffee for him and a big cup of coffee for me. We would talk about my project for hours at a time, finally realizing that we needed to stop talking when we could not hold in the coffee anymore. These were really challenging conversations for me, because my then-director is a very systematic thinker and I am not, but I had to convince him that I was making a cohesive argument. I think that the conversations were interesting to him because I came at the study of theology from a different perspective than him and used different evidence to justify my arguments.

These are three very different experiences: a sport, music, and talking theology. What are the components of these experiences that allow me to lose myself in any of them? In each case I am doing something that I really like to do, something that I find intrinsically rewarding (no one needs to tell me that I need to do any of these activities in order for me to want to do them, and I find doing them meaningful and would argue with anyone that thought they were not meaningful). They are all challenging activities but activities that I am competent enough at that I do not become frustrated. More than this, in all three cases when I would be particularly well prepared I would more often be able to enter flow. Sometimes I would take a long nap before Frisbee. On those days I would stumble around the field like a zombie. Sometimes I would not prepare good writing for my director. On those days I would leave his office as soon as possible. Some days I would not "feel" it when playing music with my friends. This would often be more frustrating than rewarding.

All three experiences also require the presence of friends that are doing the activity with me. Is it important that these people are actually my friends or would other Frisbee players or musicians or theologians also be adequate colleagues in these endeavors? I know that for myself, having friends to play sports or music with is important. If I play sports or music with people that I do not know very well, or worse, do not like, I cannot enter flow. However, I would grant that some people, perhaps very practiced and talented athletes or musicians, might be more able to enter flow if they were around similarly talented but unfamiliar performers. I suspect that this is also the case because I have really enjoyed some theological conversations that I have had with people I had never met before who are also professional theologians. My conversations with my director in graduate school were times when I would totally forget about everything except the conversation. I would forget about my hunger or my need to use the bathroom. I expect this was at least partly due to the level of challenge in those conversations. This leads me to speculate that experiences of flow might be greater when the person's competence and challenge are both higher. The things that we are best at and enjoy the most are probably the best candidates for flow.

The final experience of flow I want to share with you is a bit of a counterexample. I have played Tetris since it was available in Canada on video game consoles in the mid 1980s. One of my favorite things about playing Tetris is that it takes enough concentration and attention that I can forget other things that are going on around me for a few minutes. I find it really relaxing in this way. Many people find video games enjoyable because video game programmers are particularly adept at making playable games that hit the sweet spot between anxiety and boredom, between challenge and frustration.

Interestingly, Tetris shares very few components of the first three examples. You usually play alone. It is not an intrinsically valuable task. I play a fair amount of Tetris, but if I was asked to justify it, I would admit to being at a loss beyond the significant response that I enjoying playing. Perhaps video games are a virtual example of flow? They simulate the experience of flow but without any of the ordinary components. Jane McGonigal thinks that video games are the key to solving our world's problems. Video games give us attainable goals with the possibility of epic wins. In her book *Reality Is Broken*, McGonigal details fourteen happiness hacks that are meant to make the world a better place. If I'm right that practice is essential to becoming good at something, then paying more attention to video games and how they work is probably going to be a good thing for us to do. People tend to enjoy the practice that goes into playing video games more than other kinds of practice and they are willing to practice skills that do not seem to have an immediate payoff in order to pursue a larger goal.

Flow and the Beatific Vision

What does all of this have to do with the Beatitude, "happy are the pure in heart, for they shall see God"? I am not interested in making the argument that flow and purity of heart are exactly the same thing, but there are some similarities that are worth noticing. It is often the case that the concepts of purity and unity are connected. We noted above that in order to experience flow it is important to be able to have a relatively narrow focus of our attention. Frisbee, music, talking to someone, and even Tetris all focus our attention on a specific and clear object of attention. Even if we have a wide-ranging conversation, we are focused on our conversation partner. Our focus is pure in this way. Similarly, the Shema, found in Deuteronomy 6:4, emphasizes the unity of God, a central tenet of Israel's monotheistic faith: "Hear, O Israel: the LORD our God, the

Lᴏʀᴅ is one." This unity is often connected to what it is like to know God, and this is likewise connected to human knowledge.

The medieval philosopher and theologian Thomas Aquinas also held that all knowledge comes from God and that the best way to achieve this knowledge is in attempting to see God. To see God is to know oneself and to know the world with incredible clarity, the kind of clarity only possible through direct vision of the divine. Aquinas suggests that this direct seeing of God (or beatific vision) is the ultimate goal of human life, although it is a goal that can only be truly achieved after death. The timelessness, unity of focus, and intrinsic value of seeing God are very similar to flow. In suggesting the beatific vision as the final object of human life, Aquinas introduces important ideas for our consideration when thinking about ethics from a Greek perspective. These are the abstract nature of truth, the importance of goals for human life, and the value of contemplation as an activity.

Greek Ethics

Greek ethics is generally oriented towards a goal. We see this most strongly in Aristotle, who wrote one of the first treatments of ethics when he wrote the *Nicomachean Ethics*. Aristotle was taught by Plato, who was in turn taught by Socrates. These three philosophers lived about 400 years before Christ. While Greek influences had a variety of general effects on the Judaism of Jesus' day, we should not assume that Jesus or Paul knew anything about these three philosophers. Likewise, although many Hebrew Scriptures would have existed by their time, it is unlikely that any of these three would have any knowledge of Jewish concepts or ways of life; however, Plato and Aristotle set the stage for much of how ethics and moral thinking came to be done in Western society. It would not be too much of an overstatement to argue that Western philosophy is mostly a footnote to debates between Plato and Aristotle. Christian ethics owes more to Plato and Aristotle in terms of form and structure and as much in terms of content as it does to the writings of the Old or New Testament. Many Christian thinkers read Plato from the fourth century CE onward and Aristotle from the thirteenth century CE onward, almost as if they were Christian thinkers.

Socrates, Plato, and Aristotle all believed that happiness was the main goal of life. To achieve the good life a person should aim for happiness. Plato believed that people could best achieve this goal by living the life they were given in the most excellent way possible. Plato's ideal society was divided into three parts: the guardians (the philosophers who ruled the society through the practice of wisdom), the military (who kept order in society through the practice of courage), and the masses (who were filled with desire that they worked to calm through the practice of moderation). If I am a part of the masses who aspires to join the military, I am thinking in exactly the wrong way, according to Plato. I should instead seek to fulfill the role that I have been given in the best way possible. This is a view of society that reinforces the status quo. Plato's ideal society was based on his view of how the human person was constituted.

The Human Person in Plato

Plato believed in a strong division between the body and the soul; furthermore, he believed that material things were essentially evil and that we should seek to transcend our bodies and concentrate only on abstract realities. This is best demonstrated in Plato's analogy of the cave. In this allegory we should understand ourselves beginning in the position of the captives. The things that you think now, that you hold to be true or good, are really just as true as shadows cast on a wall by a fire. A captive who reflects carefully on their situation, who becomes a good philosopher, may free themselves from their chains and seek the fire. Upon seeking the fire they recognize that there is a greater light beyond the fire and they leave the cave entirely, finding real truth in the sunlight. Finding the truth of the sun is like being exposed to a truth about ourselves that it is hard to take. It blinds us at first, but as we spend more time in reflection, we recognize that it is in fact true. Plato suggests that everything to the left of wall one is our physical material reality.

That on the right of wall one is progressively more spiritual so that the sun is an analogy for the abstract ideal of the good.

We see here that the material world is meaningless for Plato and that spiritual reflection is the real goal for humans. Plato does not believe that this is possible for everyone, as his ideal society discussed above suggests. It is probably only the philosophers who will be able to achieve this vision of the sun. They could try to help others leave their captivity and seek the sun, but most people who have been in the position of being captive for all their lives will, upon hearing about the sun, just start laughing. The movie *The Matrix* is an excellent contemporary version of the allegory of the cave in its probing of what is real and what is possible.

Having basically dismissed, or devalued, the body, Plato divides the soul into three aspects. The three divisions are our reason (our intellectual abilities), our spirit (our drive to get things done), and our passions (desires to eat, sleep, have sex). Our reason is governed by the virtue of wisdom, our spirit by the virtue of courage, and our passion by moderation. Wisdom is the virtue of being able to use our reason in the right measure at the right time, to discern what is valuable in the available knowledge. Courage is the virtue of exercise, the right amount of spirit at the right time in order to get the job done. The aspect of our soul most related to the body, our passion, is simply moderated in Plato's thought. He believed that the less we eat, sleep, and have sex, the better; although obviously some of all of these desires need to be fulfilled to guarantee survival. Finally, these three virtues are in turn balanced by the virtue of justice. Justice is the balance between wisdom, courage, and moderation that allows us to seek happiness. Plato believes that the way to most reliably search after happiness is to focus on the form of the good.

The good is primary form in Plato's four ideal forms (good, truth, justice, and beauty). These forms are pure abstractions that give meaning to every other form that exists ideally and to all of material reality. Again, if this sounds abstract, it is. Plato's point is that real truth and real justice are not products of our own imagination or our own efforts here on earth. The abstract idea of goodness judges whether or not we are really good, just as the idea of the sun puts into context all of our ideas about fire or light or life. Our reason is wise to the extent that it knows this abstract idea of goodness. Many of the ideas that we have in Christianity about an abstract God who is far away from us in heaven and who acts as a perfect judge on our behavior stem from the synthesis between Plato and Christian thinking.

Teleology

Aristotle was Plato's student and, therefore, was strongly influenced by him in many ways; however, there were a number of aspects of Plato's thinking that were just too abstract and otherworldly for Aristotle. For our purposes, Aristotle shared with Plato a concern with excellence, ultimate truth, happiness as a goal for human life, and a version of the forms as shaping material reality. However, Aristotle's thought is much more dynamic and practical. Let me suggest a few contrasts and then talk in more depth about the final goal of human life for Aristotle, which is contemplation.

I hope that it is obvious that while Plato believes that some people can free themselves of their captivity and seek perfection, in general most features of Plato's thinking are committed to the status quo. Plato values excellence. Aristotle is a much more teleological thinker. The Greek work *telos* means purpose, goal, or end. Teleological ethics are ethics that value the end or goal most highly. The old saying, "the end justifies the means" is loosely teleological, although Aristotle would not have liked the idea of the end justifying bad action. Teleological ethics are all about pursuing a goal in the best way possible. Teleological ethics are extrinsic in that the measure of their success is outside the person. Teleological ethics are often opposed to deontological ethics, which are focused instead on a person doing the right thing because it is his or her duty. Deontological ethics are intrinsic in that a person looks inside himself to see what the right thing to do is. (At first blush Plato seems like a deontological thinker since he is much more focused on excellence in the place that I find myself; however, the orientation of all of his thinking is outside the human person.) Aristotle is

The Gift of Ethics

the primary example of a teleological thinker. For Aristotle, we do things to achieve a goal. We can have both intermediate goals and final goals.

For instance, I like playing Frisbee. My goal is to play Frisbee. I am also hungry and my foot hurts. What is the best way for me to pursue the different goals that are present here? I will enjoy Frisbee more if I eat a little something so that my hunger does not bother me. I will also enjoy Frisbee more if I attend to my foot. Can I play with it if I wrap it carefully? Do I need to see the doctor? Is the best way to play Frisbee long-term actually to not play at all until my foot feels better? In this example we see how accomplishing a final goal is made up of a variety of intermediate goals. Aristotle believes that the final goal for all humans is happiness. Why do I want to play Frisbee? Because it makes me happy. In this excerpt Aristotle makes a number of points about how virtues lead to activities:

> Virtue, then, being of two kinds, intellectual and moral, intellectual virtue in the main owes both its birth and its growth to teaching (for which reason it requires experience and time), while moral virtue comes about as a result of habit, whence also its name (*ethike*) is one that is formed by a slight variation from the word ethos (habit). From this it is also plain that none of the moral virtues arises in us by nature; for nothing that exists by nature can form a habit contrary to its nature. For instance the stone which by nature moves downwards cannot be habituated to move upwards, not even if one tries to train it by throwing it up ten thousand times; nor can fire be habituated to move downwards, nor can anything else that by nature behaves in one way be trained to behave in another. Neither by nature, then, nor contrary to nature do the virtues arise in us; rather we are adapted by nature to receive them, and are made perfect by habit.
>
> Again, of all the things that come to us by nature we first acquire the potentiality and later exhibit the activity (this is plain in the case of the senses; for it was not by often seeing or often hearing that we got these senses, but on the contrary we had them before we used them, and did not come to have them by using them); but the virtues we get by first exercising them, as also happens in the case of

the arts as well. For the things we have to learn before we can do them, we learn by doing them, e.g. men become builders by building and lyre-players by playing the lyre; so too we become just by doing just acts, temperate by doing temperate acts, brave by doing brave acts.

This is confirmed by what happens in states; for legislators make the citizens good by forming habits in them, and this is the wish of every legislator, and those who do not effect it miss their mark, and it is in this that a good constitution differs from a bad one.

Again, it is from the same causes and by the same means that every virtue is both produced and destroyed, and similarly every art; for it is from playing the lyre that both good and bad lyre-players are produced. And the corresponding statement is true of builders and of all the rest; men will be good or bad builders as a result of building well or badly. For if this were not so, there would have been no need of a teacher, but all men would have been born good or bad at their craft. This, then, is the case with the virtues also; by doing the acts that we do in our transactions with other men we become just or unjust, and by doing the acts that we do in the presence of danger, and being habituated to feel fear or confidence, we become brave or cowardly. The same is true of appetites and feelings of anger; some men become temperate and good-tempered, others self-indulgent and irascible, by behaving in one way or the other in the appropriate circumstances. Thus, in one word, states of character arise out of like activities. This is why the activities we exhibit must be of a certain kind; it is because the states of character correspond to the differences between these. It makes no small difference, then, whether we form habits of one kind or of another from our very youth; it makes a very great difference, or rather all the difference.

This account of virtues and habits and activities is similar to the account of flow that I gave above. The key difference is that Aristotle notes that we become the people we are based on the kinds of activities and habits we inculcate in ourselves. Remember, in describing my Frisbee playing in Chicago, how I talked about how competent I am in fundamental skills but that, in terms of how

Ultimate Frisbee is played as an organized sport, how clueless I am? I did the right activity with the right people in terms of learning how to play Frisbee and in terms of having a good time and even in terms of being able to enter flow. In terms of being able to play organized official Ultimate Frisbee, I did the right activity with the wrong people. They could not teach me, since as a group we did not care. This difference is very important in terms of the kind of people we become. When we learn from examples, it is important that we are learning in the right way, from the right people, and at the right time.

We are also helped by Aristotle's concept of the golden mean. Virtues for Aristotle are much more general than they are for Plato. Aristotle believes that virtues are found in the sweet spot between two comparable vices, excess and deficiency. For instance, health is a virtue found in the sweet spot between gluttony and starvation. Courage is a virtue found between foolish bravado and cowardice. Aristotle never talked about flow, but I think that he would be happy to see flow as a virtue found between the vices of boredom and frustration.

Finally, Aristotle also believes that certain activities lead more effectively to the goal of happiness than others. He suggests contemplation or study as the activity which best leads to happiness. Why study? Is this simply the influence of Plato again? I think that if we return to the example of flow and use flow as an analogy for contemplation, we can understand what Aristotle is all about in suggesting contemplation as a perfect activity. It is not only reflection on the good or study of textbooks that leads to happiness but paying complete attention to the object of any action that will result in our happiness.

SIX

Imagination

Living into the New Possibility with Christ

"Happy are the peacemakers,
for they will be called children of God."

MATTHEW 5:9

One of the most remarkable stories of a peacemaker is that of Gladys Aylward. A movie was made about her life in 1958. James Kiefer wrote this story of her life, which he distributed through email as part of a popular series of Christian biographies in the early days of the Internet before, if you can believe it, gentle reader, the web was a big deal.

> Gladys Aylward was born in London in 1904. She worked for several years as a parlormaid, and then attended a revival meeting at which the preacher spoke of dedicating one's life to the service of God. Gladys responded to the message, and soon after became convinced that she was called to preach the Gospel in China. At the age of 26, she became a probationer at the China Inland Mission Center in London, but failed to pass the examinations. She worked at other jobs and saved her money. Then she heard of a

73-year-old missionary, Mrs. Jeannie Lawson, who was looking for a younger woman to carry on her work. Gladys wrote to Mrs. Lawson and was accepted if she could get to China. She did not have enough money for the ship fare, but did have enough for the train fare, and so in October of 1930 she set out from London with her passport, her Bible, her tickets, and two pounds ninepence, to travel to China by the Trans-Siberian Railway, despite the fact that China and the Soviet Union were engaged in an undeclared war. She arrived in Vladivostok and sailed from there to Japan and from Japan to Tientsin, and thence by train, then bus, then mule, to the inland city of Yangchen, in the mountainous province of Shansi, a little south of Beijing. Most of the residents had seen no Europeans other than Mrs. Lawson and now Miss Aylward. They distrusted them as foreigners, and were not disposed to listen to them. During her second year in Yangchen, Gladys was summoned by the Mandarin. A riot had broken out in the men's prison. She arrived and found that the convicts were rampaging in the prison courtyard, and several of them had been killed. The soldiers were afraid to intervene. The warden of the prison said to Gladys, "Go into the yard and stop the rioting." She said, "How can I do that?" The warden said, "You have been preaching that those who trust in Christ have nothing to fear." She walked into the courtyard and shouted: "Quiet! I cannot hear when everyone is shouting at once. Choose one or two spokesmen, and let me talk with them." The men quieted down and chose a spokesman. Gladys talked with him, and then came out and told the warden: "You have these men cooped up in crowded conditions with absolutely nothing to do. No wonder they are so edgy that a small dispute sets off a riot. You must give them work. Also, I am told that you do not supply food for them, so that they have only what their relatives send them. No wonder they fight over food. We will set up looms so that they can weave cloth and earn enough money to buy their own food." This was done. There was no money for sweeping reforms, but a few friends of the warden donated old looms, and a grindstone so that the men could work grinding grain.

In this vignette from her life Glady Aylward seems like quite the peacemaker, and I think that she is. Entering a rioting prison court-yard, a place so violent that soldiers are afraid of intervening, is paradigmatically peaceful. Not only does it show that Aylward was able to be peaceful, but it shows that in this particularly violent situation peace could solve a conflict that violence or the threat of violence would have only worsened. Aylward's status as a model peacemaker is further demonstrated by another story that finds her escorting one hundred orphans, some only a few years old, to safety over mountain ranges and the notorious Yellow River during the Second World War.

However, another story reveals Aylward to be a peacemaker who sometimes used violence. During her trek with the orphans she happened to see an encampment of invading Japanese soldiers. At this point her loyalties were entirely with the Chinese, so she de-toured the whole group so that she could reveal the likely position of the Japanese unit to the Chinese army. The next morning the valley was soaked with blood. Not a single Japanese soldier survived, but the Chinese also suffered heavy casualties.

Does this story take away from Aylward's status as a peace-maker? Did Jesus have people like her in mind when he preached the Beatitudes? Does Aylward's role in the Chinese victory dem-onstrate her continued commitment to social stability? Is it then a story of success? Aylward did achieve her goal in that moment. Or, does it show a momentary lack of imagination in a life that is otherwise continually devoted to innovative ways of finding peace? Is it a story of failure?

Failure and success are very difficult terms to understand when we think in terms of human societies. Who wins a war? The Japanese "lost" the Second World War but, at least partly because their military was severely constrained after the war, their economy is now one of the world's most robust. The United States won the Second World War and emerged as a global superpower. The United States now spends at least forty percent of the world's total spending on the military.

The Beatitudes suggest that the peacemakers will be called children of God. We recognize this phrase as referring to all people, but Jesus' hearers would have also recognized it as the term that the rulers were given in Jesus' time. Emperors would be called "sons of God" and would often refer to themselves as semidivine. Emperor worship was popular and at points enforced in Jesus' time throughout the Roman empire. Is Jesus then suggesting that the rulers who bring peace deserve this title? Or is Jesus again upsetting expectations by saying that anyone who brings peace deserves this title? Are peacemakers pacifists or do they use force to make peace? Although I am a convinced pacifist, and am similarly convinced that Jesus was a pacifist, I am not sure that this Beatitude is neatly resolved in a pacifist direction. It is certainly the case that by 350 years after Jesus' death the idea of the soldier as a Christian peacemaker was common. In the rest of this chapter I want to probe the various imaginations of what it means to follow Christ that people employed in the first few hundred years after Christ.

Before I begin, though, a few words about imagination are in order. In order to give gifts, to follow examples, to learn paradigms, and to gain habits and virtues, a certain kind of imagination is required. To follow Jesus is to imagine what it would be like to live like Jesus. This means many different things at many different times for many different people. Imagination is such a good word for what is required of the followers of Jesus because we recognize that imagination will not guarantee a single, universal answer. Imagination exercised well in the right kinds of ways will guarantee a faithful answer, but not always a predictable one. It is a genuinely difficult ethical question to parse the very different imaginations of Christians, especially when they conflict. I think that Gladys Aylward is an incredible example of a peacemaker, but I strongly disagree with the actions she took against the Japanese that day in the valley.

Jesus

In the next big section of the Sermon on the Mount after the Beatitudes, Jesus talks about a number of laws given in the Old Testament and reimagines their meaning given his own culture. It is interesting to note at this point that Jesus never seems to want to start a new religion. He is simply trying to revitalize his own Jewish faith.

Christianity is then, in some respects, a mistake. It is the result of a conversation about the meaning of Judaism that went wrong, or was too difficult, or caused too much conflict. We don't know enough about this conversation to understand it well. We have some evidence about how the followers of Jesus, especially new followers who had not previously been Jewish (called Gentiles), tried to fit into Judaism and continue to worship Jesus. We also know that all Jesus followers joined, stayed or at least tried to stay in Jewish synagogues. The word *Christian* starts to be used only around two hundred years after Jesus dies. Our first record of it is in the letter between Roman officials trying to decide if they can kill someone for simply being called Christian or whether or not they need to do the things that Christians do. By then, Jesus followers had been excluded from synagogues and they were meeting and worshiping in houses and in other small groups.

Anyway, this section of Scripture where Jesus is focusing on these Old Testament laws and offering his own take on them is called the antitheses. In Matthew 5:38–41 we have an antithesis that deals with violence:

> You have heard that it was said, "An eye for an eye and a tooth for a tooth." But I say to you, "Do not resist an evildoer. But if anyone strikes you on the right cheek, turn the other also; and if anyone wants to sue you and take your coat, give your cloak as well; and if anyone forces you to go one mile, go also the second mile. Give to everyone who begs from you, and do not refuse anyone who wants to borrow from you."

This passage is typical of the other antitheses and like the Beatitudes there is a particular structure here. In each antithesis Jesus begins with a law, offers an intensification of the interaction that the law addresses, and then provides examples. In this antithesis the law, known as the *lex talionis* or "law of the claw," is a negative limit that attempts to contain the sin of revenge. Jesus responds with an action, generosity, that seeks to undercut the motivations behind the sin. If people act with generosity then revenge is not necessary. It does not need to enter the picture. This is another good example of the economy of the gift.

It's certainly true that this kind of generosity is difficult to practice, but it is important to remember that this is not simply letting the violent have their way with you. Turning the other cheek is certainly not cowering in a corner after being hit, or becoming purely submissive. It suggests to your "enemy" that you intend to deal with them as an equal but also that you are going to upend the expected or worldly ways of solving problems.

Throughout these antitheses Jesus is retelling the story of the Jewish people and emphasizing adherence to the spirit rather than the letter of the law. For him this meant consistently challenging his imagination to find new and different ways to perform his faith. Other examples of Jesus' imagination are found in his reliance on parables and his performance of miracles. These especially are open to many different interpretations. Rather than trying to lock meanings down, Jesus seems to be interested in having people listen to stories that challenge their imaginations; he is always pushing them to think more deeply about their faith.

The Church

Different churches have different imaginations. There are a whole host of historical, cultural, and religious factors that have led to the current situation. Giving a history of these factors is beyond the scope of our study here, but it is useful to briefly explore two moments in church history that have strongly shaped church imaginations.

The first is a shift that happened slowly over several hundred years from about 150 CE to 500 CE, but that we can understand by focusing in on the Roman emperor Constantine. In the years after Pentecost, the church grew through missionary journeys, house churches, and conversations in Jewish synagogues. The church that resulted contained both Jews and Gentiles in a sometimes uneasy blend; however, there was a clear focus throughout the church at this time. This focus was on the voluntary worship of Jesus Christ as the son of God and on following the way of Christ. In this time it was dangerous to be a Christian. Both Jewish and Roman officials persecuted Christians, and at times Christians were actively targeted for extermination. This meant that following the way of Christ often led to crucifixion for the follower, just as it had for Jesus.

In 312 Constantine "ended" persecution against Christians in the Edict of Milan. This statement guaranteed freedom of religion in the Roman Empire. In 325 at the Council of Nicea, Constantine established the Christian religion as the religion of the Roman Empire. This meant that, over time, Christians were no longer persecuted for their beliefs. Being a Christian stopped being dangerous. It also meant that, over time, being a Christian stopped being a matter of voluntary commitment. Everyone in the empire "became" a Christian.

The "Constantinian shift" was then one in which being Christian shifted from requiring a courageous imagination voluntarily committed to worshiping and following Jesus to an imagination in which worshiping and following Jesus was the established, expected norm for everyone. This shift in imagination also changed the nature of what it meant to worship and follow Jesus. The church came to represent the best moral ideals of society rather than a prophetic countercultural voice calling society to account.

The second moment in church history that demands our attention is the Reformation of the sixteenth century. Spurred on by Erasmus and Luther, the sixteenth century saw a series of reformations to all forms of Western Christianity. When the dust settled, three dominant types of Christianity emerged with three distinct imaginations. Let us briefly summarize these.

The Roman Catholic imagination had always had at the center of its faith, worship, and practice the sacrament of the Eucharist. Every mass has the Eucharist, and the high point of every mass is the celebration of the Eucharist. In this sacrament the Christian partakes in the body and blood of Christ. This imagination is very physical, emphasizing the concrete nature of our daily relationships to each other and to God. The Catholic imagination (Roman Catholic, Anglican) is one that has at its center the body of God.

Martin Luther could not make sense of this imagination. For Luther it was only an experience of God's grace that could offer salvation to the Christian. In the famous phrase "justification by grace through faith," Luther expresses the idea that the belief that humanity had been made right with God through God's grace was key. This grace was something that could be communicated through words more effectively than sacraments and, therefore, preaching quickly moved to the center of Protestant faith, worship, and practice. Protestant worship has as its high point the sermon, the preaching of the good news of God's grace. This imagination is very logical, emphasizing the need for us to hear God's grace in order to be saved. The Protestant imagination (Lutheran, Reformed, Methodist) is one that has at its center the word of God.

The Mennonite church grows out of the third type of Western Christianity, Anabaptism. The Anabaptist (or Radical) Reformation never grew numerically in the same ways as the Catholic or Protestant reformations. This is partly because Anabaptists believe that the center of faith, worship, and practice should be the community. This meant Anabaptism remained out of step with the Constantinian pattern of connecting the belief of the people with the belief of their ruler, a pattern that continued to dominate both Catholicism and Protestantism well into the twentieth century. An example of the centrality of community for Mennonites is the practice of singing in worship. Singing connects humans to each other as their voices blend together and connects humans to God as their voices rise in praise. This imagination is very relational, emphasizing the possibility of following Jesus in life without compromise. The Anabaptist imagination (Amish, Mennonite, Brethren in Christ) is one that has at its center the kingdom (or better, community) of God.

These imaginations are all very different one from another. But I believe that they are all faithful. Seeking the commonalities between them is an excellent task for Christians to undertake as they work together to discern the good life. This will happen best when we share our stories and seek to understand the different ways in which we are following Jesus.

SEVEN

Rules

Formal Ethics in Christianity

"Happy are the merciful,
for they will receive mercy."

MATTHEW 5:7

Throughout these chapters I have been emphasizing the importance of stories, self-discovery, characters, examples,
virtues, and imagination in how we pursue the good life. There
has been very little focus on practical steps that we could take to
be ethical. This is deliberate because, I am convinced, in "being"
ethical it is more important that we emphasize who we are "being"
than particular ethical rules or concepts. I remain convinced that
this is the case, and I hope that I have been able to show you that
this is a rational way to think about ethics. However, it is also true
that many people believe that ethics is more about following rules
than it is about what kind of people we are. I want to spend some
time in this chapter looking at ethics more formally than I have
until now. By "formal" I mean particular systems of thought or
approaches that shape how ethics is looked at regardless of who

we are. There are, of course, some significant advantages to this way of thinking. Rules give us discrete laws to follow and anyone can follow them. In this chapter we will probe a few of these more formal approaches to ethics, all developed by Christians.

The Beatitude about mercy, one of four Beatitudes that are unique to Matthew, is the moment in the Beatitudes where we see something that closely approximates this formal approach to ethics. Think about the relationship between the descriptive part of the Beatitudes and the gift or reward that is given. Often the gift abundantly exceeds the descriptive, as in Beatitudes like, "Happy are the meek, for they will inherit the earth," or "Happy are the pure in heart, for they will see God." Here, though, the gift is an exact replication of the action and attitude. The merciful will receive mercy. The reward in this case makes sense, and it is the kind of sense that we don't even need to be Christian to understand. This is a part of a biblical worldview that is broadly shared across many approaches to being ethical. Sayings like "You give what you get" fit well into this way of thinking. In fact, this was exactly the goal that Immanuel Kant had in framing his categorical imperative in the eighteenth century, at the height of modernity.

Immanuel Kant

Kant was seeking to guarantee the terms of human behavior by appealing to our reason. His goal was a morality that every reasonable person would agree to. Unlike Hebrew ethics, which views our relationship to a giving God as most important; Aristotle, who views our relationships to our friends as profoundly shaping; or Christian ethics, which are dependent on following Jesus, Kant wants us to be able to look inside ourselves and discover the right thing to do rationally.

Kant's focus is on reason and he is a strongly deontological ethicist. Deontological ethical systems focus mainly on our duty. Teleological ethics like Aristotle's are all about pursuing a goal in the best way possible. Teleological ethics are extrinsic in that the measure of their success is outside the person. Teleological ethics are often opposed to deontological ethics, which are focused instead on a person doing the right thing because it is his or her duty. Deontological ethics are intrinsic in that a person looks inside himself or herself to see what the right thing to do is.

The possibility of looking inside ourselves for the right thing to do requires that we are able to posit the human person as an autonomous individual. The word *autonomous* is from two Greek words: *auto,* which means unto itself, and *nomos,* which means law. The individual who is autonomous is a law unto himself or herself. This idea is especially prevalent in societies like those found in North America at the beginning of the third millennium.

The Modern Human Person

The rise of the autonomous individual, the person who feels like he or she doesn't need guidance from any outside source, is a very complicated thing to track in history, but the French philosopher Rene Descartes gives us a good place to start. Descartes, much like Kant, is eager to find a secure grounding for human behavior. Descartes lived at the end of the Thirty Years' War in Europe, a time in which society was in the process of massive change and had just experienced one of the bloodiest wars in history. Descartes wondered how he could find certainty in a time of so much upheaval. His method was to doubt everything. Once his process of radical doubt was complete and he couldn't find anything else to doubt, he would have found the answer to what is most certain. Descartes found this answer in the fact that regardless of what he was doubting, it was always Descartes who was doing the doubting. Throughout his entire process Descartes was the rational being engaged in surveying his world. The slogan for Descartes' philosophy is "I think therefore I am."

This statement is interesting in a number of ways. First, it is Descartes who is doing the thinking. Two hundred years before Descartes' time people would not have focused on the individual. In medieval and earlier Europe people thought of themselves as belonging first to a society or people or clan. Descartes doesn't say,

"The French people think therefore they are." Second, Descartes suggests that thinking is what guarantees his existence. Descartes doesn't say, like everyone two hundred years before his time would have, that belief is the guarantee of our existence. He doesn't say, "I believe therefore I am."

If we reflect on Descartes, we can see a broad change in what counts as truth and rationality. This shift is called modernity. I think we can suggest that modernity began with Descartes. This shift consists of three parts, and it is fundamental to understanding how we now think. Furthermore, understanding this shift also helps us understand some of the disconnect that we might experience between Hebrew, Greek, or early Christian ethics and our own (modern) concepts about what ethics is.

The shift occurs in three ways, in terms of how we find truth (this is a question about method), who guarantees that it is truth (or what authority do we look to to prove that it is truth), and who the truth is focused on (what is the fundamental or basic unit of society).

People gradually stopped trusting in faith as a way of knowing what was true and started relying on reason as a way to discover what was true. Even though both Descartes' and Kant's systems are very Christian in the end, they rely more on reason and less on faith to explore their world. People also gradually stopped trusting the church to guarantee truth and started looking to science. These two changes both mean that we see in modernity (roughly from 1650–1950) a rise in formal ways of thinking about ethics. What makes sense guides the discovery of ethics, not the question about how to be a good person or how to best follow Jesus. The final shift opens the way for Kant's ethics. This is the shift from people thinking of themselves as belonging first to a society or people or clan to thinking of themselves as individuals. Descartes saying "I think therefore I am" represents a shift from "We believe therefore we are."

The Categorical Imperative

The center of Kant's ethics is a basic moral rule that he calls the Categorical Imperative. Here it is as he formulated it in *Grounding for the Metaphysics of Morals*:

> "Act only according to that maxim whereby you can at the same time will that it should become a universal law."

This statement is difficult to understand, and there is significant debate among scholars about exactly what it requires in terms of human action. Here are a few things that we can definitely know about it. It is an "imperative." Whatever the statement means it is something we must do. It is categorical. Kant uses the word *categorical* differently than we might expect. Kant uses categorical as an antonym for hypothetical. Hypothetical situations are those in which if several things are the case together then something else might also be true. A hypothetical ethical rule might go something like this: "If someone gets hit by a car you should stop and help him." The person needs to get hit by the car first for the rule to come into effect. If I see a homeless person who obviously needs my help, nothing about this rule obliges me to help, unless he has been hit by a car. I need another hypothetical rule or some kind of more general rule to follow. Categorical rules must always be followed. You need to do them in all situations at all times regardless of all other variables. They are not in any way hypothetical, so we know that Kant's rule obliges us and that it obliges us all the time.

Let us look more closely at what the law says:

Act only according to that maxim . . .

This phrase has one unusual word in it. A *maxim* is a high standard or mark by which behavior is judged. It is not exactly the same thing as a goal, because you do not necessarily work towards it, although we often work to live up to a standard we have set for ourselves. (This part of the rule is open to teleological interpretation, as you might have noticed). Here Kant is simply saying that our actions should be excellent and that they should be focused in a particular way.

> ... whereby you can at the same time will ...

This phrase is more self explanatory. Kant focuses in on the will. We can see here Kant's focus on our own duty. For Kant, we look inward for the strength, resolve, and reason to live according to this moral rule.

> ... that it should become a universal law.

Finally, we get the focus of the categorical imperative. Kant suggests that our own actions should always be capable of being made into universal laws. I do not think that Kant thinks that we need to make every action into a universal law, but I do think that Kant believes that everything we do needs to be excellent enough that it should be made into a universal law. There is nothing hypothetical about the word *should* in the last sentence. The force of Kant's system is to suggest that individuals should behave as if everything they did would be agreeable to every other rational person as the right thing to do. Kant suggests that we should act in excellent ways that everyone would agree to as law.

This creates some difficult situations for Kant. First, can I now do anything I want as long as I really think that it should be a universal law? We immediately recognize that some actions need to be ruled out. No one can steal, because if everyone stole then there would be no concept of property. Stealing is parasitic on private property. No one can lie, because if everyone lied then there could be no concept of truth. Lying is parasitic on the truth. Are these extra hypothetical laws? Probably not, because we all recognize, at least everyone that is not insane (and that is exactly Kant's target market), that lying is always bad and that if people made a habit of lying, not just truth but communication itself would be in jeopardy.

Is it the case that lying is always bad? Let's say that a really big guy, who is obviously really angry, storms up to the door of my house and pounds on the door with both fists. And let's say that he has a really big gun in his hand and some knives on his belt. When I open the door to see what he wants he shouts, "Is your wife home?" Now, I know that my wife is in the back room working on some business, but do I tell the truth and tell the angry man, "Come on in,

I'll get her," or do I say, "No, she is down at the police station turning in some forms that they need. Why don't you look for her down at the police station!" I am always going to choose the second option even though it is a lie. My wife's life is much more important than telling the truth in this situation, but Kant's categorical imperative doesn't grant me any such wiggle room.

The final problem is the practicality of this law. Is it really the case that everyone everywhere can agree on what the right thing to do is in all situations? Kant believes that his system should be applicable across cultures and even across time and history. Kant's rule is very commendable because it suggests a universal, logical way to have people solve conflicts short of war, but it probably needs some adjustment in order to be feasible.

You may have noted that the categorical imperative is a lot like the Golden Rule. The Sermon on the Mount saves the Golden Rule for close to the end:

> In everything do to others as you would have them do to
> you; for this sums up the law and the prophets (Matt 7:12).

There is a key difference between Jesus' statement and Kant's categorical imperative. Jesus embeds his "rule" in the story of the Jewish people, "for this sums up the law and the prophets." Kant's categorical imperative is abstracted from any story. In fact, as we have discussed, it is abstracted from all stories, all cultures, and all histories.

Casuistry

The last system that I want to discuss here is the practice of casuistry. Casuistry has been incredibly important especially in Roman Catholic ethical thinking. It grows out of the practice of confession. When the practice of confession started, it was as a way for a church to, both before and after the time of Constantine, hold its people accountable to what it means to be a Christian. This became progressively more difficult as more and more people became Christian and especially once society was entirely Christian as it was by the Middle Ages. It became more difficult because people became more and more ignorant about what it meant to be Christian. It also became more difficult because the clergy were increasingly poorly trained. The solution to these problems was to issue manuals of moral theology. These manuals were books of sins with appropriate penances attached to them. They helped priests keep people accountable to their faith. The method involved in these manuals was casuistry. Casuistry is the identification of the good through comparison of cases. For instance, which is worse, stealing a loaf of bread to feed my family or physically attacking my brother with a knife? Since it is worse to go at my brother, I should receive more penance for that. This idea that some things are morally worse and than others has had significant effects on how we think of ethics today.

One effect is that it enlarges the scope of what can count as ethical behavior. Rather than thinking of some actions as trivial and other actions as greedy, all kinds of actions are compared and graded ethically in a system like casuistry. Actions like the fraud Enron engaged in leading up to their bankruptcy in 2001 or the shortsightedness leading up to the Deepwater Horizon oil spill in 2010 become horribly bad, but ethically relevant, actions. They are no longer dismissed as simply greedy.

Another effect is that the emphasis here shifts away from who the person is to what they have done. I think that there is a way to think about confession that sees it as an important aspect of remembering the story of what it means to be a Christian by reminding ourselves what is not Christian behavior. However, much of the casuistic side of confession has led to a formalized ethic that tries to prescribe human behavior rather than encourage human flourishing.

Rights

The final formal approach to ethics that we need to consider is based on rights. This is the dominant ethical framework in the Western world today. The history of human rights is very interesting and we learn a great deal about what rights are by thinking our way through this history. One of the first people to use the term rights was Francisco Vitoria, who argued in the early 1500s that the many different peoples living in South and North America had the right of dominion to the land they lived on. This right was natural and not human. This means that the *indios* (these native South and North American peoples) had rights to their land and their lives that were given by God naturally, and that they did not need to be given these rights by any human government or power. Vitoria thus attempted to limit the impacts of colonialism. John Locke, in the late 1600s, argued that everyone had a natural right to life, liberty, and property, and that we could transfer these rights to the government to gain more secure enjoyment of our rights. Locke was very influential on early American thinking. Note how close "life, liberty, and property" is to "life, liberty and the pursuit of happiness."

One of the first laws that sought to guarantee these natural rights in human law was the English Bill of Rights in 1689. One hundred years later, the French Declaration on the Rights of Man and Citizen was adopted. The United States Bill of Rights followed two years later in 1791. In 1948, the Universal Declaration of Human Rights was adopted. It attempted to secure rights not just in one country but across the entire world.

A great advantage of these rights frameworks is that they are *extensible.* They extend from one group of people to the next as our law and moral concern extends. Locke's life, liberty, and property was a statement of rights that could be applied to all men, or at least, all white men. In this way it was an extension of previous ethical thinking, which held that in order to have rights you needed to possess land. The point here is not so much what Locke thought but that his attention to property extended rights from one group, the landed gentry, to all men. In the United States, the extensibility of rights can be seen in an interesting way in the early 1900s, when rights started to be slowly extended from white men to women and to black men and women. This process has been a slow one and civil rights laws are still passed to guarantee these people their rights.

Part of the process has been to recognize that rights should not be taken away from people based on religion or ability or sexual orientation. Laws passed to guarantee these people's rights continue to insist on the extensibility of rights. More recently questions of extending rights have gone beyond humans to animals. Some people think that the most intelligent animals (elephants, apes, dolphins) should be granted rights. Some people think that all animals with a consciousness should be given rights. Some think that all animals should be given rights.

The key point in this discussion is not necessarily who should have rights, although I would tend to cast this net quite broadly, but rather that rights are useful because they give us ways to compare our treatment of different individuals and secure a basic level of ethical treatment.

The Human Person

However, this is also the biggest problem with rights; that they only secure a basic level of treatment. Rights language tends to *atomize*. Individuals are granted rights but only a lowest common denominator of rights. When we think about rights, we do so in a way that is concerned only to grant that with which we can provide anyone. In this way, rights are granted not according to an economy of gift, but according to an economy of scarcity. A problem with each of the approaches that I have highlighted in this chapter is the way they turn the human person into a rugged autonomous individual, disconnected from stories with thin, if guaranteed, rights.

EIGHT

Righteousness

Filling Our Hunger

"Happy are those who hunger
and thirst for righteousness,
for they will be filled."

MATTHEW 5:6

Immediately after college I held a job as a youth pastor at Charleswood Mennonite Church, in Winnipeg, Manitoba. This was the congregation where a number of my professors attended and a variety of other church leaders were also members there. After about two months I received a call from a First Nations person who needed some groceries to make it until his next paycheck.

I was eager to help and I talked to the lead pastor about the appropriateness of diverting a small amount of my budget for the youth to this man. My pastor agreed that, if I felt this was important, I could do it. I met the man at a grocery store and shopped with him. He left the store with around thirty dollars worth of groceries. He did not make all of the choices that I would have made, but I was proud that I did not choose to judge. I drove him home to a part of Winnipeg that I had not been in often and said my goodbye. He expressed genuine gratitude that my church had been able to feed his hunger.

I was so eager to help because I had learned in a new way in college about how badly First Nations peoples had been treated. (In the United States we typically use Native American to refer to the indigenous population of South and North America. Other terms are used in other countries and in Canada, my country, we used First Nations while I was living there. This term was preferred because it insisted both that these people had been here first and that they were still, under the law, sovereign nations.) I knew the details of this treatment from my high school education. I grew up in Kitchener, a city that has sprawled into a number of surrounding communities to create a contiguous settled area of more than half a million people. My ancestors were some of the first Europeans to move to this part of the world. Only a generation or two removed from Europe they moved from Pennsylvania right after the British government forcibly removed all of the First Nations people from the area. Kitchener and most of the surrounding communities are situated close to the Grand River. In 1784, the Haldimand Proclamation granted six miles on either side of the Grand River, from its source to its end, to the Six Nations, a grouping of First Nations people who allied with the British during the American War of Independence. This is about one million acres. By 2000 about fifty thousand acres were recognized as Six Nations land. My father's ancestors moved close to Kitchener, well inside the Haldimand Proclamation, fifteen years after it was issued.

So I knew in an abstract way that the land I grew up on was in important ways stolen. But when I moved to Winnipeg I actually met First Nations peoples. A group was protesting on the grounds of the provincial capital in Winnipeg. They had erected a giant teepee and were encouraging supporters to come down every evening to be a part of their protest. It was the nicest protest I've ever attended. We sat around, talked, and listened to drumming, and after a while danced a traditional circle dance together.

In Kitchener I had always felt a distinct sense of guilt about where I was born. In Winnipeg I felt forgiven.

I tell this story, as the last one I will relate to you in this short book, because it is a good example for me of the Beatitude this chapter begins with. In Kitchener I hungered and thirsted for righteousness, but only a little bit. It would probably be more accurate to say that I considered hungering for righteousness, but often opted for something else instead. It was almost as if I hungered for a burger but often ate pizza instead. In Winnipeg, partly because the menu was broader and more available, I was able to hunger for righteousness. And I was able to be filled. In order to be ethical we need to know why we want to be ethical but we also need to put ourselves in situations and places where we can be ethical and around people with whom we can be ethical.

And so I was eager to help the man who called me for groceries.

This meant that I was all the more disappointed when an elder from my church reported to me that he had learned that the groceries I'd bought were being sold for money to buy drugs and alcohol. He knew this because he knew the area of town that I rarely went to, since he had spent his whole career working with First Nations people. He worked for justice for them, to see that their needs were met, and he had a good connection to many people in the community. He knew that the particular groceries that I had helped purchase were being used as money in this way.

I learned many lessons from that situation. I learned that you cannot always control the consequences of your actions, but that action always have consequences. I learned that it is always good to help people, but even the best help is beyond our control. That is, we cannot shape or control perfectly how our actions will be used. I also learned that the best gifts are given inside a relationship that already exists. My anonymity allowed for my help to be, in my mind, misused. If the elder had given the help it would have been *received* in a very different way because it would have been received inside a relationship, and inside a community.

Righteousness in Matthew 5:6 is much like shalom. It is a state of relationship to God that people work for together. Righteousness happens inside a covenant. It happens when we use God's gifts well. It happens when we give good gifts to each other and when we learn how to use these gifts well. It happens when the very difficult work of living inside an economy of gift, and economy of covenant to God, is a challenge that we take up together, practicing and developing habits that lead us into the kingdom of heaven.

The rule of accountability in Matthew 18 is perhaps the best example of how people might work together as they seek to discern the best version of themselves:

> "If another member of the church sins against you, go and point out the fault when the two of you are alone. If the member listens to you, you have regained that one. But if you are not listened to, take one or two others along with you, so that every word may be confirmed by the evidence of two or three witnesses. If the member refuses to listen to them, tell it to the church; and if the offender refuses to listen even to the church, let such a one be to you as a Gentile and a tax collector. Truly I tell you, whatever you bind on earth will be bound in heaven, and whatever you loose on earth will be loosed in heaven. Again, truly I tell you, if two of you agree on earth about anything you ask, it will be done for you by my Father in heaven. For where two or three are gathered in my name, I am there among them." Then Peter came and said to him, "Lord, if another member of the church sins against me, how often should I forgive? As many as seven times?" Jesus said to him, "Not seven times, but, I tell you, seventy times seven."[1]

This weekend I went to the thirty-fifth anniversary of Chicago Community Mennonite Church. This congregation has formed my belief and practice deeply. We engaged in several times of storytelling over the weekend, listening and remembering the ways in which we have walked together over the last thirty-five years. Our church was one of the earliest congregations in the Mennonite Church USA to welcome people as members regardless of sexual orientation. The teaching position of the Mennonite Church USA—the national denomination—is that homosexual practice is sinful, but there is an acknowledgement that it is a question around which much disagreement exists and that we should continue to

1. With "seventy times seven" I am here using a possible alternate reading of the text.

listen to all those interested in talking about the questions and stories surrounding sexual orientation. The position of my church (we call ourselves CCMC because our whole name is a mouthful) is that there should be room in the denomination for a congregation of people who together hold the minority position.

CCMC did not seek out this minority position. It happened to us, probably partly because of our urban location, because people who we recognized as Christian were asking for membership but had the "wrong" sexual orientation. The pattern of accountability listed in Matthew 18 that starts with two people talking and then has larger groups talking and finishes with whole congregations talking happened again and again over about a fifteen-year period at CCMC.

It began inside the congregation. After a time we decided that sexual orientation was not, for us, a valid criteria for membership. Some people left and this was painful; new people came and we rejoiced.

It extended to our area conferences (we belonged to a conference in Illinois and another overlapping conference in the Midwest) as people in those conferences learned of our discernment and found it challenging.

In the Illinois Mennonite Conference the conversation became very tense and difficult. In that case the larger conference decided to discipline our congregation for a practice that went against their discernment. In this case we were on the outside of the pattern of accountability listed in Matthew 18. We did not become exactly as Gentiles and tax collectors, but there were actions taken against us. We wanted to remain in relationship with our sisters and brothers in the conference and so we chose a group of four people who took on the work of continuing to talk to the conference. This hard work went on for years.

And then, all of sudden, we got a letter from the conference. It was a full apology for how they had participated in conversation with us. Leaders in the conference took responsibility for a discernment process that was less than ideal and invited us back into full fellowship with them. They had not changed their mind, but they did not think that we were surely wrong either. There are a number of assumptions about the rule of accountability in Matthew 18 that I want to highlight in conclusion.

In order for this rule to work people must already be connected to each other. For Christians this happens in baptism. For Mennonites, baptism happens as an adult so a voluntary choice is made to join the church. The importance of voluntary baptism is to highlight the person's choosing to be bound to the community in discerning the best way forward. I did not have a way to discern the best way forward with the man to whom I gave the groceries. We did not have a prior relationship. He did not attend my church. I have often thought since then that the failure in that story was not so much in his choosing to sell the groceries (although that was surely a bad decision), but in my choosing not to seek out a relationship with him once he had initiated it with me by asking for money. Perhaps I was the one who refused to receive the gift of a relationship with him.

In order for the rule of accountability to work people must be open to making a decision together, but also to expecting that they might not end up where they began. This happened both to CCMC when gay men started to attend our church and to the Illinois Mennonite Conference when they realized that the conversation they had started with CCMC did not have a predictable ending. In explicitly Christian language, we must be open to the Holy Spirit.

Finally, notice how the whole rule is dependent upon the economy of gift. Peter wonders how often he is called to forgive, and Jesus responds in an unexpected way. Not just seven times or seventy times but seventy times seven! Infinity plus one.

My point has not been to end this book with a story about sexual orientation but instead to end with a story about accountability, baptism, forgiveness, and abundance. These are the practices that make us the people who can learn how to be good. They are the way that we can confront difficult issues gracefully, finding out who we are and who God wants us to be. Our only decision is to be righteous and to expect that we will be filled.

Bibliography

Aristotle. *Nicomachean Ethics*. Indianapolis: Hackett, 1999.

Austin, J. L. *How to Do Things with Words,* 2nd ed. Cambridge, MA: Harvard University Press, 1975.

Bratsiotis, N. P. "Nephesh." In *Theological Dictionary of the Old Testament,* vol. 2, edited by G. Johannes Botterweck and Helmer Ringgren, 316–32. Grand Rapids: Eerdmans, 1974.

Geirland, John. "Go With The Flow." *Wired*, September 1996, 4.09, 160–61.

Janzen, Waldemar. *Old Testament Ethics: A Paradigmatic Approach*. Louisville: Westminster John Knox, 1994.

Kant, Immanuel. *Groundwork of the Metaphysics of Morals*. Cambridge: Cambridge University Press, 2012.

Kiefer, James E. *Gladys Aylward: Missionary to China*. http://justus .anglican.org/resources/bio/73.html.

McCabe, Herbert. *Law, Love and Language*. London: Bloomsbury Academic, 2003.

Williams, Rowan. "Making Moral Decisions." In *The Cambridge Companion to Christian Ethics,* edited by Robin Gill, 3–14. Cambridge: Cambridge University Press, 2001.

CPSIA information can be obtained
at www.ICGtesting.com
Printed in the USA
LVHW041329090819
627124LV00001B/59/P